EAU CLAIRE DISTRICT LIBRAR
6528 East Main Street
P.O. Box 328
EAU CLAIRE, MI 49111

W9-AXA-425

Finding Your Passion

WITHDRAWN

"This book will help you organize your search for the right career for you. A career that will make you excited to get up every morning because of what you get to do today. The practical advice, uplifting stories and convenient checklists and forms throughout the book provide a great, easy to follow road map. If you use this process, you'll identify a more rewarding career path, and outline the specific actions you need to take to get that great job!"

Joe Twohig, AVP,
Video Operations, Jobing.com (www.jobing.com)

"Finding Your Passion" will not only guide you to career success and happiness professionally but will also assist you in your personal growth as well. This is a book that you will want to read again and again because once you find your dream, you will need to execute the principles of this book to achieve your goals."

Sally M Luck, Director of Human Resources, KUSI-TV

"If you know there is something more for you in this lifetime but you just can't seem to uncover what that is, this book is a must read. Designed specifically with an itinerary to capture one's true desires, Finding Your Passion offers the clarity we all seem to need."

Saundra Pelletier, (www.saundrapelletier.com),
Author of "Saddle Up Your Own White Horse"

"Finding Your Passion" is not only inspirational, but also truly helpful. Marcy Morrison gives you real tools to help you break past whatever has been stopping you from fulfilling your dreams. This book is helpful for people in any stage of their lives and can be read and used over and over again!"

-Jordanna Petkun, Founder/CEO of Emerge Art Center

"At a workshop Marcy presented to members of the Junior League of San Diego, I was amazed at her talent for taking us through the exercises detailed in this book. They are simple to execute, but yield strong results. In a group of volunteer women who thought we knew each other well, by using Marcy's tools like developing a 'spin', we learned new things about one another. And more importantly, we were able to take this new knowledge and make further connections we didn't even know we needed! As a woman leaving a 12-year career following the birth of my twins, Marcy's training & this book have been valuable tools to help me find my new passion as a Mom and a Volunteer. The hardest part is not identifying what my "new" passion really is, but rather gathering the courage to make that search. Marcy's enthusiasm and knowledge helped me overcome the nerves and fears and are helping me take the next leap!"

Tina Campbell, President, Junior League of San Diego

"To excel in life one needs to be on purpose. Once you are on purpose, life is magical and you attract all you need to succeed. Marcy shows the way - a must read for all who are seeking their purpose in life."

Azim Khamisa (www.azimkhamisa.com)
Author/Speaker/Peace Activist.
"Bounce Back: Secrets of a Bulletproof Spirit"
by Random House

Marcy Morrison is truly passionate about helping others live their best life through fulfilling, passion-filled work. "Finding Your Passion" is essential reading for anyone who knows that they can live their ultimate purpose through their career, but needs to find the right road to accomplish their dreams.

Vivian Glyck, Founder,
Just Like My Child Foundation, (www.JustLikeMyChild.org),
Author of "Tao of Poo: Keeping Your Sanity (and Your Soul)
While Raising A Baby" and "12 Lessons on Life I Learned from
My Garden: Spiritual Guidance from the Vegetable Patch"

"Finding Your Passion" is THE book you must read if you're ready to live your full potential and identify exactly HOW to do so!"

Tami Walsh, M.A., President,
Teen Wisdom, Inc. (www.teenwisdom.com)

""Finding Your Passion" is a powerful combination of practical tools and inspiring anecdotes that calls the reader to action. The exercises found inside lead the reader on a personal journey to paint a vivid picture of your dream career and realize the resources already in place to begin its pursuit. "Finding Your Passion" is a catalyst for searching deep to discover and develop hidden goals and confront and resolve deep seeded fears that would prevent us from achieving them. Because the reader finishes the process with a hard copy of this experience, it can be referred to over and over again during times of struggle as a motivating reminder of your innermost passions and the legacy you want to leave behind."

Adam Roark, Director, Business Development,
Ensure Charity (www.ensurecharity.com)

"Over my career I have been fortunate enough to meet and work with a large number of incredibly successful people. I found that they all had one thing in common, they love what they do! Surprisingly uncovering your passion and purpose may not be as simple as you think. Marcy Morrison's book is full of inspiring stories but more importantly it gives you the tools to help you discover what you truly love to do. Once you discover your true passion she then gives you proven techniques to find a job that will inspire you, energize you, and allow you to do great work. I believe Thoreau was correct when he wrote "The mass of men lead lives of quiet desperation." Too often we let outside influences from society, friends and family dictate what we do with our lives. All too often the end result is unrewarding job and a less then satisfying life. Shake yourself free from the expectations of other people by taking the time to read this book, and use its tools, you will be glad you did."

Michael Montsko, President,
Weichert Lead Network (http://www.weichert.com/)

Marcy has illustrated effectively how to navigate your job search and vocation. Her stories, steps, and experience helped me better understand the rewards associated with finding a dream job. She inspired me and will compel you to think and act "outside of the box."

– **Liam Dunfey, COO,**
University Advisors Admission Specialists
(www.UniversityAdvisors.net)

"Finding Your Passion is full of sage advice, powerful exercises, and inspiring stories that will put you on the road to your dream job. Marcy is a great guide and a great coach. She makes it easy. Dive into your dreams with this book."

Patrick Combs Author, "Major In Success"

Finding Your Passion

The Easy Guide to Your Dream Career

MARCY MORRISON

New York

EAU CLAIRE DISTRICT LIBRARY

T 144945

Finding Your Passion
The Easy Guide to Your Dream Career

Copyright 2009 Marcy Morrison. All rights reserved.

No part of this publication may be reproduced or transmitted in any form or by any means, mechanical or electronic, including photocopying and recording, or by any information storage and retrieval system, without permission in writing from the author or publisher (except by a reviewer, who may quote brief passages and/or short brief video clips in a review.)

Disclaimer: The Publisher and the Author make no representations or warranties with respect to the accuracy or completeness of the contents of this work and specifically disclaim all warranties, including without limitation warranties of fitness for a particular purpose. No warranty may be created or extended by sales or promotional materials. The advice and strategies contained herein may not be suitable for every situation. This work is sold with the understanding that the Publisher is not engaged in rendering legal, accounting, or other professional services. If professional assistance is required, the services of a competent professional person should be sought. Neither the Publisher nor the Author shall be liable for damages arising herefrom. The fact that an organization or website is referred to in this work as a citation and/or a potential source of further information does not mean that the Author or the Publisher endorses the information the organization or website may provide or recommendations it may make. Further, readers should be aware that internet websites listed in this work may have changed or disappeared between when this work was written and when it is read.

ISBN 978-1-60037-545-3

Library of Congress Control Number: 2008910465

MORGAN · JAMES
THE ENTREPRENEURIAL PUBLISHER

Morgan James Publishing, LLC
1225 Franklin Ave., STE 325
Garden City, NY 11530-1693
Toll Free 800-485-4943
www.MorganJamesPublishing.com

In an effort to support local communities, raise awareness and funds, Morgan James Publishing donates one percent of all book sales for the life of each book to Habitat for Humanity. Get involved today, visit **www.HelpHabitatForHumanity.org**.

Acknowledgments

Thank you to Jennifer Burstedt and Karli Bobus, both students from the University of California, San Diego, who believed in me and told me that my service of working with students was incredibly valuable and much needed. They were the inspiration for me to create my business.

Special thanks to Kristin DiBacco, who helped me understand the 20-something market and was generous with her time to help me market and sell my work. Also thanks to my personal cheerleaders, including Rob, my husband, who is the technical genius behind my website and continues to be supportive during every step along the way. Thanks to my dad, Herb Honnold, who provided me with a business loan to get my ideas off the ground. A big heartfelt gratitude to my two children, Cameron and Logan, who inspire me everyday and, by being a mom, allowed me to do some soul searching and uncover the next phase in my dream career.

Thanks to the people who boldly and bravely pursued their passion and shared their stories: Dominic Catalano, Joe Sweeney, Sally Estrada, Eric Seastadt, Paul Lamb, Vivian Glyck, Bill Hagey, Stella Medina, Scott Kyle, Jordanna Petkun, Michael Spengler, Azim Khamisa, Donna Pinto, Tami Walsh, Stephanie Malcolm, Steve Wasson, and Sally Martin.

Heartfelt gratitude to Marci Shimoff and Janet Attwood for sharing their words of wisdom; to my Jobing.com friends Todd Covelli, Joe Twohig, Rosanna Indie, and Dave Carns, who put me on the front lines of helping job seekers with speaking engagements, videos, and a blog; to my incredible Mastermind team: Sarah

Granby, Tami Walsh, and Jordanna Petkun; to Heather Shepard for her brilliant and strategic mind; to Donna Pinto for her outstanding editorial skills and vision; and to Joe Sweeney for being an incredible mentor. Also thanks to all of the people who helped me along the way and were also my other personal cheerleaders: Sally Estrada; my mom, Mary Jo Kenny; my stepfather, Paul Kenny; Vivian Glyck; Allison Oster; Tracy LeRoux; Sara Cloostermans; Jeremy Martin; Kathy Krasenics; Mark Fackler; Tiffany Cleary; Paul Cleary; Paul Lamb; Amy Elkind; Jannine Meyerott; Carrie Wasson; Ruthi Bozman-Moss; Katharine Kubichan; Becky Candra; Lynn Reineman; Tamar Elkeles; Tamiko Biagioli; Sally Martin; Laurie Ward; Armin Afsahi; and Lauren Hasey.

Special thanks to my literary agent, Bill Gladstone, and to Ming Russell of Waterside Productions, Inc., who believed in me and found a great home for my book with Morgan James Publishing. Thank you to David Hancock and his team at Morgan James Publishing for also believing me and helping me produce an outstanding book that will inspire and help many people to find their dreams.

Thanks to Jack Canfield and his book *The Success Principles: How to Get from Where You Are to Where You Want to Be* and The Success Principles Coaching Program, which truly helped me have the courage to take a leap of faith to be an entrepreneur and to stretch to achieve mind-blowing goals. Thank you to John Wood and his book *Leaving Microsoft to Change the World*, which instills hope and inspiration that anything is possible when your heart is in the right place, you follow your gut, focus on solutions, and dream big.

Dedication

To my mom, who instilled in me the desire to love and to learn about other cultures and to travel the world

To my dad, who taught me the impeccable values of honesty, integrity, fairness, and being highly organized

To my children, Cameron and Logan, who continue to inspire me with their innate ability to find joy, fun, and adventure in every day

To my husband, Rob, for always believing in what I could achieve and for supporting me even when I didn't believe in myself

To all the incredible family and friends who have come into my life and have provided me with incredible gifts of wisdom and knowledge

To all of you, who have a dream inside and trust that you can achieve all that your heart desires

Contents

Attention: Your Dream Is Waiting!

"Success is not the key to happiness. Happiness is the key to success. If you love what you are doing, you'll be a success."

—Albert Schweitzer, humanitarian

Introduction

After many years of working with others to assess their career goals, it became clear to me that everyone has a dream inside. All that you need is assistance in unlocking and uncovering that dream, along with some guidance and empowering tools to get you on your journey to finding your dream job, career, or business. You also need someone, or multiple people, who can serve as your personal cheerleader(s) and support team to help you stay excited and enthusiastic about your dreams and remind you to continue to believe that anything is possible. When you are in touch with what you are passionate about and are able to market and sell your skills, you become a magnet that attracts the necessary resources that will help you find your dream. You just need a guide who will ask you the right questions to uncover your passion, talents, and dreams. You want to feel uplifted, empowered, and inspired to achieve your goals.

I created my company, Careers with Wings (www. careerswithwings.com), to help individuals find their passions and develop their personalized strategies for success. In response to feedback from my workshops and one-on-one sessions, I recognized a need for a powerful yet simple book that provides a kick-start to finding your dream career. I kept recommending that my clients read other career- or success-related books. The feedback I continually heard was, "Way too long—way too overwhelming." Many felt disempowered even before they began. Instead, most said they wanted a more interactive, fun, inspiring, uplifting, easy-to-use book or workbook with exercises that could guide them to unlock their passions and find or create their dream career. Through workshops and one-on-one sessions, I discovered that individuals felt most empowered by being asked thought-provoking questions. *Finding Your Passion* offers the best exercises and processes from real-world career strategy sessions and workshops. Pulling from my own experience and knowing how other people's stories have often been the catalyst for change in me, I have included inspirational and motivational stories of courageous people who followed their passions and are successful, sometimes against all odds.

I firmly believe that we get in touch with what we are meant to do when we come from a childlike sense of play and fun. When we are in this state, we create an environment that is more conducive to opening us up to opportunities that will lead us to our dream job. *Finding Your Passion* will also help you cut out the outside noise so you can truly get in touch with who you are meant to be and what you are meant to do. The easy-to-use exercises simplify the process by helping you gain clarity and put together a focused plan. You will feel motivated and inspired to work through *Finding Your Passion*, instead of sticking it on a shelf where many books end up. Also, I have created easy-to-use tools and resources that are accessible on my website, www.myeasycareerguide.com.

Three symptoms *Finding Your Passion* will alleviate include the following:

- Feeling overwhelmed and not knowing where to begin—This guide helps you have a place to start and keeps the process simple, and it will give you empowering tools to help you move forward and find your dream career.
- Lack of excitement and enthusiasm due to being worn down by the job search process—By keeping it simple and clarifying your passions and strengths, you can be filled with energy and enthusiasm again.
- Loss of self-confidence and self-esteem in the job search—By working through the exercises in this book, you will build up your confidence and self-esteem by teaching you to believe in yourself, trust your gut, and remember to focus on your strengths. You also will build a support team to bolster you up during tough times.

Throughout life it is common to have multiple passions, passions that continually evolve and even change with time. Ever since I was an exchange student to Australia during my last year of high school, I have been passionate about international work. I have lived, worked, and studied all over the world. Now as a mom of two young children, I am still passionate about international work; however, I have had to reassess my priorities because a career that requires heavy international travel would not allow me the time that I crave with my children. In reexamining my passions, I realized that I absolutely love helping individuals uncover their own passions and then working with them in strategizing a path that leads each person to his or her dream job. This is something I had been doing in a volunteer capacity for many years and kept receiving feedback that I should start my own business. I decided to turn that feedback into action by creating Careers with Wings. It has been an incredibly rewarding journey to see the shift in people's lives as they gain clarity on their passions and create their own personal road map to attain their dreams.

I also realized that I could keep my passion for international work alive through volunteering efforts. I presently serve on the advisory board of the Just Like My Child Foundation (www.justlikemychild. org), an organization working in Uganda. I know that I can make a difference in many other ways as well, which I strongly believe is my responsibility as a global citizen.

Your own assessment or reassessment can come at any point, and even at multiple points in your life, including these times:

- In high school, when examining where you want to go to college and what you want to study
- In college, determining the best internships or jobs that are in line with your passion
- After a couple of years in the workforce, when you are clearer on what you enjoy, and even don't like, doing
- During a major life change (i.e., becoming a parent, getting a divorce, moving, or realizing that you have been in your job for many years and are burned out and ready for a change)
- In your current job, when you want to reignite passion for what you are already doing
- When you retire and want to consider what to do with your newly found free time and possibly pursue a passion that may have been put on hold for many years

Finding Your Passion will guide you in these areas:

- Identifying your passions and strengths
- Providing you with tools to market and sell your skills
- Strengthening your ability to trust your gut and believe in yourself

- Developing a support team
- Learning how to network
- Enhancing your current job
- Creating a personalized plan for success
- Enjoying and trusting your journey

Finding your dream career is an incredibly exciting journey, and I wish you all the best as you embark on yours. Please do not hesitate to contact me if I can assist you in any way. I'd love to hear your success stories and anything else you would like to share.

Make sure you take the time to visit my website, www.myeasycareerguide.com, to take advantage of the resources and support available.

Wishing you a life filled with dreams come true,

Marcy Morrison
La Jolla, CA
www.careerswithwings.com
www.myeasycareerguide.com
marcy@careerswithwings.com

"Laugh often, dream big, and reach for the stars."
—Anonymous

Chapter 1:
Uncover Your Passion and Strengths

"When your heart speaks, take good notes."
—Judith Campbell

Before we get started, I highly recommend finding a friend or someone else that can serve as an accountability partner. You can both work through *Finding Your Passion* together and serve as each other's personal cheerleader and help each other find your dreams. Take the time to work through the exercises; they are critical to helping you uncover your passion.

Let's begin your journey to finding your passion and your dream career. It is never too early or too late to pursue what you are passionate about doing. Do what you want to do by finding a way to make it happen.

Potential Challenges to
Finding Your Passion and Dream Career

- Making sacrifices
- Getting additional training
- Doing extensive research
- Taking a leap of faith
- Finding a mentor or coach
- Working two jobs
- Faking it 'til you make it
- Being bold
- Believing in yourself, even when others think you are completely insane
- Mustering up the courage
- Being strong in the face of rejection
- Walking away from it all to do something completely new
- Stepping outside your comfort zone
- Stretching yourself
- Doing what you and others thought was impossible
- Taking risks
- Following your heart
- Blocking out the outside noise
- Hitting a lot of walls and learning to walk around them
- Going the extra mile

So, are you ready to uncover your passion? Believe me, it is worth it to live *your* passion. Why is it worth it? How would you feel if you could live like this:

- Jumping out of bed each day with energy and enthusiasm, loving what you do
- Don't even feel like what you are doing is work

- Being so fired up about what you are doing that you attract people and resources as if you were a magnet

The key to finding your passion is to do what *you* want to do—not what your parents, society, friends, significant other, or anyone else wants you to do. Get clear on what you are passionate about doing—your vision of why you are here on this earth—and become the expert on marketing and selling your skills. I can say with all sincerity that when you are genuinely passionate about what you are setting out to accomplish, your energy and enthusiasm will attract the necessary resources and people you need to find your dream career. Also, discovering what you are passionate about serves as a compass that will keep you on track to arrive at your destination.

This process is truly an opportunity to do some heavy soul searching and to take time to look into your heart. One day, this question came to me, "What does my heart know that my mind does not?" Often, our heart gives us direction that does not make logical sense to our minds, but I believe that your heart is a better guide that will lead you to your dream. Take the time to listen and follow your heart when answering the questions throughout this book.

So often we go into autopilot and follow the course we think we are supposed to be on—go to college, get a job, et cetera. We don't take the time to stop and think, "Is this still working for me?" Or even better, "Has this ever really worked for me?" Well, I commend you for picking up *Finding Your Passion* and taking the time to stop and reevaluate where you are and discovering if this is really where you want to be.

Let's start the journey of uncovering what *you* really want to do and how to make it happen. Now is the best time to start living your dream.

It's Never Too Late to Pursue Your Passion

Dominic Catalano started off his college experience by studying radio and TV, but, as he was in the middle of his studies, life threw him a curve ball. His father had a stroke and quadruple-bypass surgery, and he had to drop out of college to manage the family businesses. Originally, he intended to do this only for a few years. However, almost twenty-five years later, he found himself still in the restaurant business. Dominic and I met to discuss how he could return to his passion of radio and TV and be truly happy with his work. We first had to walk through his fear of leaving behind something that he knew so well. The more we spoke, the more it became clear that Dominic was aware that life is short, and it was time for him to truly start living his passion. So with a leap of faith, Dominic sold off his businesses and started his own video production company, Lasting Memories Family Tree Video (http://www.lastingmemories-ftv.com/). Dominic shares that he feels alive again and looks forward to getting up every day to live his dream.

Why is it so important to uncover what you love to do and then to make it happen? There are lots of answers, but first and foremost is happiness, just as my client realized in the story above. I would highly recommend that you read Marci Shimoff's book, *Happy for No Reason*, and I wanted to share with you these quotes from her book:

> The research on happiness clearly shows that people who are deeply committed to whatever gives their life meaning are much happier than those who don't have a greater sense of purpose.

> When you're clear about your passions, you're lit by a fire inside that shows you what to do in each moment.

Completing the following exercises will help you get a clearer picture of what your passion is and what your dream career looks like.

Take the time to really dig deep and soul search about what you want to accomplish in life. Look at the big picture and how this next career step will fit into that and get you closer to accomplishing something bigger. Often when we explore our career in terms of the contribution we want to make in life, it lights a bigger fire inside of us than just thinking in the short-term.

What kind of legacy do you want to leave on this earth?

If today were your last day on earth, what could you say were your proudest moments, both in your career and your life?

If today were your last day on earth, could you say that you accomplished all that you wanted to accomplish?
What else is there to accomplish?

What Do You Love to Do?
Be honest with yourself.
Right now, are you living your passion or someone else's?

Do you know what your passion is?
If so, what is it, and are you living it?

What truly makes you feel excited?
What kind of work would make you jump out of bed with
energy and enthusiasm, ready to start your day?

Describe your perfect work day/month/year (e.g., your duties, activities, where you work, your travel opportunities, whether you are working in a team or alone)?
Assume that money is no issue.

Describe your favorite job(s) and why? How did you feel?

Describe your worst job(s) and why? How did you feel?

I do my best work when ...

EAU CLAIRE DISTRICT LIBRARY

When are you the happiest?

What did you always dream about doing when you were a child?

What would you do if you believed that anything is possible?

What is something that you do or would do even without pay because you love doing it so much?

**Where do you volunteer?
Often people are living their passion
via their volunteering activities.**

**What do you like about your volunteering?
What specific activities do you like the most?**

Journal about your discoveries from these questions:

Evolution and Further Discovery of Passion

A lot of people are concerned that they may not have their passion clearly defined. The truth is that we all continue to change and evolve. You have to start in the direction of what interests you. You can more clearly define your passion as you acquire more experience.

You may find it challenging to truly soul search in the same surroundings that you have been in for a long time. I find that a lot of people who are really lost and need to do some soul searching have amazing discoveries when traveling either domestically or internationally. When we are outside of our familiar setting and comfort zone, we are forced to grow and uncover who we truly are and what we love to do. You may want to consider researching opportunities that will remove you from your comfort zone to truly allow you to stretch and grow. You will see a wonderful example of this in Stella's story in an upcoming chapter.

If you feel like you need to do further digging to uncover your passion, I highly recommend *The Passion Test: The Effortless Path to Discovering Your Destiny* by Janet Bray Atwood and Chris Attwood (http://www.thepassiontest.com). The Passion Test will provide you with easy to use and powerful tools to get clear on your passions and live them. It also provides inspirational stories of people who have lived their passions. *The Passion Test* defines passion as "the inner fire that propels you forward through the love for what you're doing and the inner sense of purpose that comes from connecting to one's deepest passions. Enjoyment arises from this combination of love and purposefulness." I also love this quote from *The Passion Test*, which is definitely in alignment with the stories provided in *Finding Your Passion*, "Even if there is no one who has ever done what you are passionate about doing, there is abundant evidence of people who have been successful doing what others thought was impossible."

What's Stopping You?

A lot of the time, when we write and talk about our fears, they lose their power. I remember when I was feeling completely miserable in a job; my husband first told me, "You have to remember this is only a job—there are plenty more out there." Then I expressed my fear of leaving, and he said, "Really, Marcy, ask yourself, 'What is the worst that can happen?'" I thought to myself, "Really, what is the worse that can happen? Yes, it's true it may take me awhile to find another job, but I know that I will find one." Looking at these questions straight on, I realized that the worst that can happen really isn't something that can't be overcome. This is such an empowering question, and I often ask this to myself. What I realize is that when I talk or write about the worst that can happen, it often reveals itself to not be so scary after all, and solutions begin to present themselves.

Why are you afraid of taking a leap?
What is the worst that can happen?
Examine your fears and solutions in the following exercise:

Example:
Concern: What if I end up hating the leap that I take?
Possible Solutions: There are more jobs out there—you can always change.

What are your "worst-that-can-happen" scenarios?
See if you can come up with a solution or solutions
that makes taking a leap not so scary.

Concern:
Possible Solution:

Concern:
Possible Solution:

Concern:
Possible Solution:

Concern:
Possible Solution:

Concern:
Possible Solution:

Now it is time to shift your focus after walking through the fear. Take the time to think about all of the wonderful possibilities. What is the best that can happen?

Example: I find something that I am absolutely passionate about doing that allows me to work the hours I want, et cetera.

Finding Your Strengths

Take into consideration that all of us are naturally talented in certain areas. Examine what comes naturally to you and where you excel. Leveraging your strengths and your passion are the keys to overcoming the hurdles that you will inevitably encounter on your journey. For example, one of my clients kept focusing on the fact that she was not formally educated, but when I met with her, it was clear that her experience and personality more than made up for her lack of formal education. We worked on focusing on her many strengths. Once you are clear about your strengths, you will be more confident in marketing and selling your skills.

What do others see as your strengths? Often, we are too close to our strengths because they are such a part of who we are that we don't see them as strengths.

Action Item: Send an email to your top twenty friends and colleagues and ask them to share with you what they see as your top five strengths. Offer to do the same for them if they are interested. You'll be amazed by what others see as your strengths, and it may provide you with a secret key that leads you to finding your passion.

**What are your findings? What are your top strengths?
List them here:**

In this exercise, I don't want you to overthink the following questions. Put down what first comes to your mind—what your heart and gut know, not your head. Your head will try to rationalize and use logic to move you away from your dream. When answering the questions below, think about your bigger picture answers and how what you want *now* fits into your bigger vision.

Top five list of what you would like in your dream career (i.e., location, type of work, pay, activities):

1.

2.

3.

4.

5.

Top five list of what you have to offer in your dream career (e.g., skills, personality, what makes you unique):

1.

2.

3.

4.

5.

Fill in this chart below with photos or words from magazines or elsewhere of your dream job and life (if this area is too small, feel free to use a bigger piece of paper or poster board):

Where are you living?	What types of people are you surrounded by?
What are you doing (include both work and fun)?	**Anything else fun and exciting?**

For a downloadable form of this worksheet, please visit www.myeasycareerguide.com.

Dream Career

Take all of the information that you have put together above and summarize your dream career (i.e., where you work, how you feel, what you are doing, and where are you living).

Create a News Article About You!

Write an article of you being recognized for the amazing work that you do in your dream career. Make it look real by looking at your favorite newspaper's website or print layout and formatting it to look like that. Project out ten years from now and create a visual picture of how you want your dream career to look. For examples, visit www.myeasycareerguide.com.

Chapter 2:
Trust Your Gut, Believe In Yourself, and Find A Way To Make It Happen

How many times have we stopped short of achieving our dreams because the outside voices (society, our family, etc.) and our logical voice say we are crazy? Make a choice now that you won't let anyone, including yourself, tell you that your dream is not possible.

In the last chapter, you clearly identified what truly makes you feel excited and what kind of work would make you jump out of bed with energy and enthusiasm, ready to start your day. Trust what answers come to you and go in that direction. There are many people who will tell you that what you want to do isn't possible. We get so stuck by the idea that we have to follow a traditional path to achieve our goals.

> **Things You Will Hear
> When You Take a Leap of Faith**
>
> - That's not the area you studied.
> - You don't have the right credentials.
> - You don't have the right contacts.
> - You've already invested so much in your current career.
> - You're too old.
> - You're too young.
> - It's impossible.
> - It's a recession.
> - It's too competitive.
> - You're crazy.

Does that sound familiar? Learn how to block out that negative noise and keep moving toward your dream. You have to believe in yourself despite the odds. You'll be inspired by the people in the stories that follow who learned these steps and practiced the principles highlighted throughout *Finding Your Passion*, including trusting their gut, marketing and selling their skills, networking, building a support team, and working their plan. Many of them didn't follow the traditional path. In fact, many of them can be described in this way:

- Are living their dreams against the odds
- Walked away from a comfortable path
- Took a leap of faith
- Followed their hearts
- Didn't have the right credentials
- Discovered their passions in some of their darkest moments
- Blazed their own trail
- Were bold and courageous

- Believed in themselves despite all of the naysayers
- Faked it 'til they made it

Achieving Success in All Areas of Your Life

As we discussed earlier, while being a huge success in your career is a lofty goal, having success in all areas of your life is really much more fulfilling. Joe Sweeney is a wonderful example of creating success in all areas of his life and is someone who regularly practices the principles highlighted throughout this book. Joe is multifaceted and lives a multidimensional life. There aren't many people I know that can manage as much as Joe can from a business perspective and still take time to be an incredible husband, friend, and father to four children, not to mention staying in top shape. Joe's list of skills are instrumental to his success: a strong belief in himself, an ability to think big, business acumen, an incredibly high-level of energy, charisma, a belief in others, a strong ability to motivate others, outstanding networking skills, respect for others at all levels, a commitment to excellence, honesty, and integrity.

Joe grew up in a family of small business owners in Wisconsin, where owning your own business was always discussed and where Joe learned hard work and passion from both his parents and his eight older brothers. While he did try a stint in a corporate environment, it became clear to him early on that he was meant to work on his own. Being an all-state basketball player and having a huge love for sports, it was also evident to Joe that he wanted to find a way to combine his passion for sports and business. While receiving his MBA at the University of Notre Dame, Joe served as the director of sports marketing and promotions for the university's athletic department and also set out to achieve his goal of owning his own business. Not one for doing anything on a small scale, combined with having a high tolerance for hard work, boundless energy, and a burning desire to never work at a corporation, Joe was determined and focused to figure out how to own his own company. He spent more than two years in the university's library, manually compiling a list of about thirteen hundred small midwestern companies with retirement-age chief executives. (This was before computers and databases.) With the help of someone he hired to represent him, Joe developed a creative sales pitch of why these companies would want to hire a successor like Joe. He sent letters of inquiry to all thirteen hundred businesses and received about eighty responses. One of those responses turned into a job with Pipkorn Steel, a steel fabrication firm. A short time later and with help from Pipkorn's owner, Joe purchased Arkay Corporation, a Milwaukee-based photographic equipment manufacturer. Later, Joe sold Arkay for his first million dollars at the age of thirty, a goal that Joe clearly envisioned when starting out.

Another key component of Joe's success is that he realized early on how important it was to develop a support team. Due to the loneliness he experienced as a small business owner, he began to network at cocktail parties. Through networking, Joe developed the art of what he calls "compassionate curiosity," where he would express a strong interest in learning about others. Through these conversations he developed lifelong business relationships and friendships. As a result of his networking and breadth of knowledge, Joe has been served on twenty-three boards and has been invited to serve on over one hundred. From these relationships, he formed a group of twelve people, who now comprise his support team and are what he calls his "wingmen." He uses the term wingmen as it is truly meant— someone, male or female, who will watch your back and be willing to take a bullet for you. Joe also believes that we are all people and that no one is above or below him and gives respect to all people. This has allowed Joe the ability to connect with some incredibly highly successful people, including one of his main wingmen, Craig Leipold, the owner of the Minnesota hockey team, the Wild, among other successful business ventures. The wingmen provide Joe with perspective and help him foresee issues that he may not anticipate by himself. Joe states that not everybody can be your wingman or wingwoman. You need someone that would be willing to take a bullet for you, so chose carefully when making your selection. At the same time, Joe is an outstanding wingman to many people, including those represented by the many boards where he plays an active role.

Regarding networking and meeting key people, Joe is very clear about which five people he'd like to talk to at an event. He creates a business agenda and then approaches these people in a subtle way. He also likes to stretch himself and be open to learning something new by meeting one or two people that he hadn't planned to meet. He basically has no fear when it comes to meeting new people and attributes this to being the ninth son and having to be able to assert himself in a big family. We will discuss both building a support team and networking in further detail in the following chapters.

Since Joe sold his company, he has owned and operated six other companies, and again, he has interwoven sports throughout his career. One of the companies that Joe created was a sports marketing firm representing numerous professional athletes, including three-time National Football League (NFL) MVP Brett Favre. In addition, Joe was president of the Wisconsin Sports Authority, recruited and oversaw NFL training camps in Wisconsin, and was instrumental in getting the 2002 Major League Baseball (MLB) All-Star game in Milwaukee. Currently, Joe heads an investment banking firm in Milwaukee, which is involved in the $190 million sale of the National Hockey League's Nashville Predators. Joe also serves on six boards, is the chairman of his sports marketing firm, and is an equity investor in a number of companies. As a testament to his impressive sports background and connections, enterprising spirit, business acumen, drive, enthusiasm, and interpersonal skills, Joe was recently short-listed to be the president of the Green Bay Packers.

It is important to note that Joe balanced all of these achievements with almost always being home for dinner to be with his wife and kids and took a regular part in his children's lives by coaching little league and basketball for fifteen years, among many other activities. While he realized he may have sacrificed achieving even more financially so he could be with his family, he never regrets the time he spent to develop successful and well-rounded children, who are now all grown up and out of the home. Joe also regularly makes himself available in the community and is always there to help a family member or a friend in need. Joe is so passionate about helping others that he is working with a sportswriter to help him with his fitness goals. At the same time, Joe is dedicated to his own health and wellness and works out six times a week. At fifty, he is as fit as some guys in their twenties. As someone committed to continued self-development and growth, Joe is an avid reader and stays young at heart by being open to trying new things at any opportunity he can.

Joe's Tips for Both Life and Career

- Follow your passions—they arise from your heart (goals are only things you achieve). Passions are the loves of your life.
- Ponder. When you are gone, how do you want to be remembered?
- The key to life is not being smart or rich or beautiful or right. The key is to adjust to what life gives you. It is *how* you adjust—how fast and how sensitive—that will make all the difference.
- Feel you are an integral part of the whole—not just in your business or your family, but in the human race. Feel like you can make a difference by living.
- Make the best of your circumstances. No one has everything and everyone has something of sorrow intermingled with the gladness of life. The trick is to make the laughter outweigh the tears.
- Set clear goals.
- Compartmentalize. Be focused on the task at hand.
- Be persistent. Don't give up at the first challenge.
- Have determination.
- Wake up each day happy to go to work.
- Do the rocking chair test when you have a decision to make—ask yourself, if you don't do the decision, will you regret it when you are 95 and reflecting back in your rocking chair?
- Have a back up plan so you don't need to be anxious when moving forward with decisions.
- Maintain balance in your life every day.
- Put in the time to make your goals happen.
- Learn to ask good questions. It is more important to ask good questions than to have all the answers.
- Be selective. Pick and chose who you spend time with, events you go to, and how you spend your time.
- Don't watch too much mindless TV. Instead, be committed to learning by reading and trying new things.
- Practice compassionate curiosity.
- Strive for success at the speed of balance.

Joe's Tips for Both Life and Career (cont.)

- Success leaves clues. Study successful people.
- Always hold yourself accountable and accept responsibility for your actions.
- Never flinch at failure. If you are not making mistakes, you are not doing anything.
- Look at problems as challenges and opportunities.
- Surround yourself with wingmen/wingwomen.
- Be a strong wingman/wingwoman for others.
- Avoid negative people and negative anchors.
- Spend the majority of your waking hours in the now.
- Wake up happy and go to bed happy.
- Smile and laugh a lot.
- Greet everyone with a smile and a positive outlook.
- Go into the future for planning and into the past only for evaluating and learning.
- Brick walls are there for a reason. They are not to keep us out. The brick walls are there to give us a chance to show how badly we want something. The brick walls are there to stop people who don't want it badly enough.
- Be straight with people. People can handle unpleasant certainties better than we can handle pleasant uncertainties—people just want to know.
- Don't take yourself too seriously. Don't think that somehow you should be protected from the misfortunes that befall others.
- You can't please everybody and don't let criticism worry you.
- Think less and produce more.
- Give more than you receive.
- Network.
- Take time for others.
- Exercise. Regular workouts give Joe enormous energy to achieve all that he does.
- Look at the options presented to you and ask yourself, "Is this a 'Hell, yes' or a 'Hell, no'?" Pick the "Hell, yes's."
- Life is short. Live life to fullest.
- Live in an attitude of gratitude.

Has Your Passion Changed or
Has Life Led You Down a Different Path?

Many people get stuck in jobs that are no longer where they are meant to be, or they pursue a career in an area that they studied out of a sense of obligation and not out of a place of passion. Are you finding yourself passionate about something other than your major in college or in an area where you are working now? Don't fret. It is more important to follow your passion than to force yourself to work in a field that you are now less passionate about.

One of my clients made a big career transition from being a scientist with two master's degrees in biology to trying her hand at finding a position in human resources (HR). Though it was daunting to tell her friends, family, and supervisor, it was amazing how supportive the people around her were once she told them she wanted a career change. People who helped her through it included students that had made a change before her, career coaches, and individuals she held informational interviews with to learn more about their jobs. One great lesson she discovered was that it is important to keep your options open in the process of determining which jobs might fit your interests, personality, and talents. That said, it is also important to look right under your nose at your hobbies, interests, and volunteer positions. Though it was a long and challenging process for her, she knew she made the right decision right away when she talked to her boss about changing careers and then woke up the next morning without any regrets. She did find her dream job in her new field and celebrates that everyday.

Once you put yourself out there as someone looking for a full-time position working with people (or whatever you desire), things begin to happen. Do what you love, what you would do for free—volunteer work, for example—and opportunities might arise from there. This client's volunteer work not only helped her to wake up and realize she loved her extracurricular activities much more than her graduate studies, but it opened doors for a new job in a new career direction much more suited to her passion of helping people directly.

I can speak from my own experience. During my growing-up years, I had always visualized myself as a veterinarian, given my strong love for animals and a desire to help them. However, I had a wake-up call that even though animals were my passion, science was not. I realized this as I attended my first year of college and was so disillusioned that I dropped out in the middle of my first semester. At the time, this seemed like the end of the world, but it actually was one of the best things that happened to me. I decided to regroup and go to community college and work. It was during this time that I uncovered my passion. I realized that during my year abroad in Australia, I absolutely loved living in another country, since it really allowed me to grow as a person. While Australia was not that culturally different from the United States, I loved being surrounded by other exchange students from all over the world, who greatly impressed me by their ability to learn a new language. At the same time, I found it fascinating to learn about their cultures. This set me on my journey to study international affairs and Spanish and to live in Spain, where all of my coursework was conducted in Spanish. I thrived in this environment and in these studies because I was completely in alignment with my passion. You can see more about my international work in my biography at the end of this book.

Fake It 'Til You Make It and Be Bold For Success

A lot of people have said to me, "It is not in my personality to be bold." Well, it's time to start faking it 'til you make it, because the bolder you are, the better chance you will have of finding your dream career. At first, it may seem awkward, but as you start to experience victories and get more practice, it will become easier and easier. For those of you who are more introverted and being bold is out of your comfort zone, ask yourself the simple question that we explored earlier, "What is the worst that can happen?" You may say, "I may make a complete fool of myself." The honest truth is that you might, but I can tell you that anyone who has ever been successful in anything has made a fool of himself or herself and made mistakes on the journey. Making mistakes is all a part of the process and is an excellent opportunity to learn and grow. On the other hand, think about what is going to happen if you don't make some bold moves—nothing. That's right—nothing. Now let's think of what can happen if you do make a bold move. You may receive the golden key that unlocks the door to your dream career. When you are being bold, it is crucial to think about the possibilities, not the obstacles.

Another important component of being bold is to act as if you are, or "fake it 'til you make it." One way that I do this is that I think of other people who have done incredibly courageous acts and overcome enormous odds. I was very inspired by reading Jack Canfield's *The Success Principles*, where he shares many stories of people that accomplished incredible feats by being bold. I often put those images in my mind to help me walk through the fear and take a leap of faith. If you know some people who you really admire for their boldness, talk to them and ask them for their secrets.

Also, it is easier to be bold if you have thoroughly done your research on a person, company, or event before you take your leap. The more you know, the more confidence you will have. At the same time, sometimes opportunities appear unexpectedly and you just need to take a leap on the spot. In those moments, it is important to not overthink it and to go for it, as you will see in the story that follows. You have to spend time each day visualizing what you really want and going after it with energy and enthusiasm. Learn to let the rejection slide off of you and shake it off and focus on the next opportunity to be bold.

Sally Estrada is the perfect example of truly putting herself out there, taking risks, and believing in herself. She knew that she wanted to translate her many years of practicing yoga and her training into becoming a yoga teacher. While she knew that a lot of yoga studios required many years of teaching to be hired, Sally didn't let that deter her. She knew that she already had what it took to be an amazing yoga teacher, even without years of formal teaching. Then one day, when a yoga teacher failed to appear in class, Sally boldly and courageously stood up in class and stated, "I am a yoga teacher and if you are OK with it, I will teach this class." Well, everyone was game and her class was a huge success. Not only that, she was hired by the facility to teach a regular class, even without years of official teaching. Lesson learned—if an opportunity seems out of reach by some limiting belief we hold, take a risk and put yourself out there. Believe in yourself and what you can do. The truth is that Sally is naturally a quiet and introverted person, but when she stood up, she thought of her bold friend Tomas. "What would Tomas do in this situation?" Sally thought to herself. "He would go for it," and that is exactly what she did.

Go After Your Dream with Gusto, Despite the Odds and Opposition

A lot of us have excuses—reasons why we can't find our dream job. To serve as inspiration, I would like to share the story of Eric Seastedt, who is not finding any excuses, and—believe me—he could find many of them to not live his dream. Eric suffers from a rare, debilitating disease called Méniére's disease, which can strike at any time with severe dizziness and basically left him in bed for six months in 2007. What amazed me about Eric was that he never complained and instead greeted the day with a positive attitude. He also continued to do his job, where he works on harnessing the vitality of the private sector to address the health problems of low-income and vulnerable populations in developing countries. At the same time, Eric was there the best he could be for his wife and three young children.

Eric has made a choice to not let his disease stop him from living his fullest life and making an enormous difference in this world. In 2008, Eric, his wife, and their children packed their bags and moved to Ethiopia for two years so Eric can serve as Chief of Party for a ten million dollar USAID targeted HIV prevention program.

Eric could have taken a more practical career path with his top-notch experience working with Sony, Gateway, and Intel, among other companies, but instead, he decided to leave high-tech and follow his passion for international development. Sure, it was a stretch financially, especially in supporting his family, but they are all behind him and all believe in his dream.

Also, Eric wanted me to share that it is OK to change your career path if you realize that it is not your passion. Eric wasn't afraid to walk away from a career in accounting. He was honest with himself and realized accounting was not for him. In fact, it made him miserable. He again took a bold step and applied for the Peace Corps in Bolivia, instilling in him the desire to be involved in international development.

Eric is an inspiration to me and I hope he serves as one to you. Stop giving yourself excuses why you can't have your dream job—go for it!

Blaze Your Own Trail

"Do not go where the path may lead, go instead
where there is no path and leave a trail."
—Emerson

Paul Lamb could have jumped on the dot-com bandwagon back in the late '90s but decided to take a different path. He chose to not take the plunge into the world of high-tech startups like so many of his peers. Instead, he decided to leverage technology in a different way by helping to start a small nonprofit organization then called Street Tech (now Stride Center—www.stridecenter.org), which is dedicated to training low-income and underserved youth for careers in IT.

Looking back, he recalls feeling conflicted upon seeing many colleagues become instant millionaires with stock options while he was chasing a fistful of dollars to get his nonprofit organization off the ground. Many of the companies he momentarily dreamed of working for back then have long since disappeared, but the Stride Center survived the downturn and remains a vibrant community model to this day.

More importantly, the organization has now trained over eight hundred disadvantaged individuals, and a majority of those graduates have since worked in successful careers as computer technicians. Many of the program's graduates have gone on to get additional training and a college-level education. The organization has even started its own business that puts graduates to work directly as technicians in a community-based computer repair, network support, and refurbishment operation.

During eight years in community-based technology work, Paul has been fortunate enough to witness numerous amazing feats. He has seen the formerly incarcerated, the poor, and the jobless thrive in an environment where they were cared for, exposed to cutting edge technologies, and trained for living-wage jobs.

He was reminded of one student, a great grandmother and former crack addict who had never turned on a computer before coming to the Stride Center. She eventually became a highly skilled computer technician, passing several extremely challenging certification tests in the process. Her tearful words at a graduation event, with three generations of her family in attendance, still echo in Paul's ears, "If only my druggie friends could see me now!"

Paul remembers thinking to himself then, "If only my dot-com friends could see me now," as a tear rolled down his cheek. And at that moment, it became crystal clear that he had indeed made the right choice by trading stock options for life options.

As he watches the technology industry's wild roller-coaster ride and sees new big-money opportunities come and go, he just has to smile. He smiles because he no longer feels the need to respond to the siren call of technology profits. For Paul, there is no longer any question of which path to take, and in fact, Paul is currently the principal of Man on a Mission Consulting (www.manonamission.biz), a strategic consulting firm dedicated to helping companies, foundations, and nonprofit organizations leverage information technology for the social good. Paul's forward-thinking approach is frequently sought out in the media; he serves as a radio commentator and OpEd contributor on technology and social issues in a variety of publications, including NPR's *Marketplace* and on CNET.com. He is a former fellow with the ZeroDivide Foundation and is currently a Next Generation Fellow with the American Assembly at Columbia University.

Paul's Principles

- Live in gratitude. It keeps you present and focused on the important stuff. Paul keeps a "gratitude diary," where he lists what he is grateful for on an ongoing basis.
- Be an investor. Think of your time, energy, and work in the same way as you think of stock and bond purchases as increasing the value of your money. Don't just get along; be an investor in your life!
- Give even when you don't think you can. There is a karmic law to giving (when you do it without any expectation of return and when you can least afford it) that returns goodness and happiness in ways you can't possibly imagine.
- There is only right now and soon. Obsessing on what hasn't gone right in your life or what could or should have been will get you nowhere. Putting your positive focus on what is and what you want moving forward will get you everywhere.
- Let go. Oftentimes the more you try to tightly control your life, the less things actually come to pass. The ability to let go of things, trusting that things will take their natural and best course, is a forgotten art of success.

Follow Your Heart

Vivian Glyck had what many people would think is a dream job. She worked as a marketing consultant for clients such as Dean Ornish and Deepak Chopra, and at the time, it was Vivian's dream job. But life decided that she had a bigger calling. Being a mom, Vivian found herself being drawn to helping other children to have a better life.

Through a trip to Senegal, West Africa, she was led to Uganda and the Bishop Asili clinic in Luwero, where she met an incredible woman, Sister Ernestine Akulu, who was doing an amazing job of taking care of the community with very limited resources. Vivian saw that she could help this community, which was in desperate need of a generator, doctors, educational facilities, and microfinance initiatives. Many lives were being lost to malaria, HIV/AIDS, and other diseases.

Originally Vivian had no intention of creating a nonprofit, but as she began to share her story with her friends and community, the support for this community in Uganda came flooding in, and Vivian established the Just Like My Child Foundation (www. justlikemychild.org) to directly support the Bishop Asili clinic and its community.

While this is not where Vivian ever saw herself going, she is truly grateful to have found an incredible dream—one in which she is saving and improving the lives of thousands of people in Uganda. The beauty of it all is that she has used her persuasive marketing skills to fulfill her heart's passion of serving others, as well as creating a very successful nonprofit that continues to deliver on its promises to provide solutions to issues of health care, education, and microfinance. While Vivian didn't have a complete blueprint to follow as she began and continues to build her nonprofit, what she relies on is her complete joy in knowing that she is improving so many lives. Her energy, enthusiasm, and passion is a great example of how that is the key to success. While she has made some sacrifices to live this dream, Vivian knows they are well worth it.

Finding Your Passion in Challenging Times

Ana (a pseudonym) experienced severe postnatal depression for almost a year after the birth of her first child. While many could see this as the darkest times, and in many ways it was, Ana can see the wonderful gift that this brought to her. During her depression, she would regularly meet with a therapist and look at this woman in complete awe and admiration and say to herself, "This is exactly what I want to do some day."

Being from Europe and surrounded by multiple languages, Ana always thought that she would teach French, but this challenging time in life revealed to her a different passion that she would have never discovered. When her son was one year old, she took a GRE course over the summer and decided to take small steps to pursuing her newfound passion in counseling by enrolling in one class that fall. The following semester, the spring semester, she took two classes and found out she passed her GRE exam and was accepted into the master's program. Just after her son turned four, she graduated with a master's degree in counseling. She was so in tune with what she was doing that she made it happen by being completely present with her son during most of the day and doing her schoolwork at night when he was asleep.

When her second child arrived, Ana stayed home for a year and then focused on obtaining internship hours to become licensed in Marriage and Family Therapy. She is now working twenty hours a week and has the ideal balance with two children. Ana finds her work deeply fulfilling and says it is a way for her to maintain her self-confidence and balance.

Do You Really Need Credentials?

Bill Hagey's passion for marine biology started at eight years old, when he made a deal with his dad that he would take care of the new saltwater aquarium in the living room. After struggling with this daunting process at such a young age and killing a lot of fish in the process, he gradually learned to master taking care of the aquarium. At fifteen, he decided it was time to expand his horizons, and Bill started working at Scripps Aquarium in La Jolla, California. He would work after school, caring for fish in the large display tanks. After years of looking out of the window of his house over to Scripps Aquarium and growing up watching Jacques Cousteau, a job in marine biology was something that Bill always dreamed of doing.

Also at young age, he loved building things out of paper. Later, as he learned, he built with balsa wood, fiberglass, and machined metal, and then he brought it all life with electronics. For Bill, there was nothing more magical than watching a concept become real in his own hands. However, when it came to college and trying to get the necessary credentials for his dream job, Bill struggled with trying to follow the traditional path of powering through four years of college. This path was challenging for Bill and often he didn't do well academically; he was even rejected from a program that he dreamed about attending. He kept beating himself up because it didn't come easily for him. During this time, he experienced some self-doubt that perhaps he wasn't smart enough. At the same time, Bill was following his passion for marine biology and, via his work with Scripps, he joined a company that his friends had just founded. Bill took an active part in building this company and became a partner. He kept being pulled back and forth between school and work—because society says you need the degree. But he kept saying, Wait, I already have the job I love that normally you would need the degree to have.

Eventually, Bill took a deeper look at his interests and realized that he'd like to marry his passion for marine biology and his love for building things. He realized that a marine engineering degree would suit him better. However, after struggling to get halfway through with a marine biology degree, he was not about to start over. Instead, he switched to liberal arts studies and decided to teach himself the skills he needed. He was so conflicted that he ended up dropping out of college three or four times before finishing.

After years as a partner, Bill knew that he wanted to be on his own and started his company, Pisces Design, twenty years ago. He was captivated by a customer's vision of being able to put cameras and sensors on seals and other marine creatures to study their hunting and to track their migration patterns. Eventually he and his customer (Dr. Randall Davis) deployed these all over the world, including in northern California, Australia, Antarctica, Russia, and Trinidad and Tobago. Bill definitely was living the dream he envisioned watching Jacques Cousteau growing up and has adventures that some people only dream about, including expeditions to Antarctica.

An interesting twist in the story is that Bill's first customer was from the very school where he was rejected to attend to study scientific instrumentation—yet that this is exactly what he ended up doing. While biology courses did help him, the most amazing part of Bill's story is that he did not let having the right credentials stop him. He followed his passion, and a lot of what he learned is self-taught. Bill also shared that his challenging school experiences and the lack of an engineering degree motivated him even more to prove to the world that he could succeed despite not following the traditional path. He had a dream and went after it wholeheartedly.

Bill was very fortunate that he was surrounded by key employees who helped him achieve his dreams, as well as had financial backing from family members who also believed in his dream. He also realized that he needed to prove himself to potential customers through his work and reputation alone.

Today Bill continues working on his passion by contracting through the National Science Foundation via an instrumentation development grant through the National Science Foundation and working with his partner at Texas A&M to develop and innovate ever smaller cameras and data collectors.

Travel the World and Discover Yourself

Stella Medina was studying to be an elementary school teacher; however, she found that the travel bug took a hold of her. She caught this bug when she initially started traveling around the United States after high school, then later traveling around Europe. On her travels she would find herself wanting to experience more and learn more about new ways of life. She found herself really starting to question her life choices and herself. She asked herself, "How can I continue to travel while still being able to support myself and remain independent?" She decided to leverage her experience in teaching to help her achieve her dreams. It occurred to her that she could teach English to non-native speakers and see the world at the same time.

Stella was also inspired by the book *Tales of a Female Nomad* by Rita Golden Gelman, a story about a woman living as a nomad and her journey traveling and living in different countries around the world. It made the idea of living abroad and traveling more real for her. It was inspiring to think about being able to live as a modern-day nomad, with no permanent address and living with only the things that fit in her backpack. It was exciting for Stella to think of doing something different and a new challenge for her to take on.

In her early twenties, Stella went to Thailand to be certified to teach English to students whose first language is not English and to get her TEFL certificate, an internationally recognized qualification. This was her first long trip away from family and friends and her first trip traveling alone. Fortunately, she had a couple of weeks to travel with a friend to get acquainted with the country, language, and people before she started an intensive, four-week program.

Once she was on her own, she was really put to the test, traveling alone, meeting new people, finding a job, living in a new country, and submerged in a very different culture. Thailand was her big test. She knew living on her own for six months would force her to decide if this was this was the right lifestyle for her, and it was! She fell in love with the county and settled right in, meeting other people along the way who were just like her and wanted to travel and explore the world. For Stella, this was the first time that she really knew that she was making the right choice. To have the support of other expatriates and to be able to listen to their experiences traveling and teaching was a huge inspiration to her. While in Thailand, she worked and saved enough money to take time off and travel to Cambodia, Malaysia, and Indonesia.

After Thailand, Stella returned back to the United States to work for the summer. She sold all of her belongings to save as much money as she could so she could travel again. She made a commitment to herself that this would be her career and her life, traveling and teaching in a new country each year.

Currently, Stella is finishing up a year living and teaching in Ecuador. She is in love with the simplicity that comes with this way of life. She makes enough money to survive and she is grateful for this and all of the little things in life. She doesn't experience the pressure to have a big house, a nice car, or designer jeans. For Stella, living and experiencing the world is priceless. Every place where Stella goes, she learns so much about herself, the culture, and the country that she couldn't have learned otherwise.

Before coming to Ecuador, Stella didn't know much about this small county in South America that is often overlooked for bigger, more commercial countries like Brazil, Peru, and Argentina. After spending a year in Ecuador, working and traveling all over the country, it will always hold a special place in Stella's heart. She plans to continue teaching in Latin America so she can work on becoming more fluent in Spanish.

Stella will continue to travel and teach as long as she can since she is truly aware that this is her calling. People often see Stella as brave for traveling as a single woman, but she does not see herself as brave but simply as a person following her dreams and doing what she wants and loves to do. Stella shares that having the support from family and friends has been important on her journey. When she first decided to take this path, her family thought it was a phase and that she just needed to travel and get it all out of her system. When they discovered how truly happy she was living this lifestyle and was sticking to it, they have given her all their support and love. They are so proud of her for actually following her dreams. She feels that so many people have dreams and talk about making them come true, but to actually be doing it is such an amazing thing for Stella. She admits that there are times when it gets hard to be away from your family and the people you love the most. However, her friends and family are always there to encourage her to move forward with the best lifestyle for herself. Stella is also fortunate to have the support of other traveling teachers like herself, who understand what it is like to live in new country, meet new friends, learn about new cultures, and have a true passion to see the world. Stella is discovering amazing places and experiencing things that she could have never imagined experiencing in her life. She keeps a blog of all of her travels so that someday she can look back on all of the fantastic journeys she has been so fortunate to take.

Still in her twenties, Stella has traveled to more countries and has experienced more than some people do in their lifetime. She never regrets not following the traditional path; she knows it will always be there should she decide to follow that in the future.

Driven and Focused to Succeed:
Navigating a Richer Life

Scott Kyle was driven to succeed at an early age, pouring over biographies of successful people to learn what attributes allowed them to thrive. What he learned was there were three main characteristics that successful people embodied:

1. They found something they were passionate about doing.
2. They had the natural skills.
3. They practiced hard work and put in their time to become a success.

In the course of his childhood, Scott practiced these principles through his passion for sailing and even developed spreadsheets recording his goals. At age eleven, he set himself a goal that he would be a world champion sailor in ten years and beat that goal by two years. Part of practicing the principles of successful people meant that Scott did whatever it took to succeed, including breaking the ice on a lake in the Chicago suburbs in the middle of winter to sail. His success translated to many areas of his life by continuing to focus on the three principles. Scott won another world championship in sailing, along with nine national titles. He is also an Ironman triathlon finisher and a third-degree black belt in Shaolin Kempo.

Early on, Scott described his success as vertical and very individually focused. He only felt fulfilled when he achieved his given objective. Later, Scott broadened his sense of success, which included enjoying the journey and being out of his comfort zone, even if that meant that he didn't always win. He also realized that he could attain more success if he could break out of his introverted shell and reach out and connect more with others. Scott found this new definition of success to be much more fulfilling than just focusing on attaining a goal and now laughs at himself, saying that he has lived life backwards—he was too serious in his formative years and now he interjects much more fun and enjoyment into his life. Scott shared one example of when he practiced his new definition of success. After reading that fewer people had swum the English Channel than had climbed Mt. Everest, Scott decided that would be a challenge he would like to surmount. Being dedicated to fitness and staying trim, this goal really put Scott out of his comfort zone by having to put on fifty pounds of body fat to protect him from the cold when swimming the English Channel. While he didn't complete the English Channel journey and didn't win the "gold star," he greatly enjoyed the experience that allowed him to stretch himself, meet incredible people, and learn a great deal along the way.

Beyond his sporting passions, Scott also realized that he had an enthusiasm for both economics and finance. Determined to become successful in these fields, Scott attended top schools: Tufts University for degrees in economics and international relations, the London School of Economics for a general course degree in international relations, and Harvard University for a master's degree in business. After his studies, Scott focused on gaining a breadth of experience from financial analysis to financial publishing to equity investing while working and living in the financial hubs of New York and Chicago. Due to his extensive knowledge and experience, Scott has also served on nearly twenty for-profit and nonprofit boards.

While Scott was being groomed to run a 300-person company in Chicago in the mid 1990s, he took a moment to reflect on what he really wanted and focused on a greater, richer life in all senses of the word. He kept finding himself in San Diego to soak up the sunshine and take advantage of his love for outdoor sports. Scott always felt great and energized while he was in San Diego. While some perhaps thought he was insane to leave a high-profile job, Scott felt like it was time for him to take a leap of faith and find a more enriching, balanced lifestyle.

Upon moving to San Diego, Scott combined his passion for both sports and finance by purchasing an interest in and becoming CEO and publisher of Triathlon Group North America, LLC, the parent company to the world's largest triathlon publication, *Triathlete*. Post acquisition, Scott led a team for the subsequent year that returned the magazine to profitability. Scott served on the company's board of directors until he sold his interest in the magazine seven years later.

After his stint at *Triathlete*, Scott again combined his love for finance and sports by co-founding The Active Network, Inc., which was named one of the top 100 fastest-growing companies in North America by *Inc.* magazine in 2006 and the 15th fastest-growing company in North America by Deloitte & Touche (2006 Fast 500). Scott served as CFO and as director of the board for Active. Today, Active has over two thousand employees worldwide.

Currently, Scott runs Coastwise Capital Group, LLC, where he continues his passion for finance/money management, practices the principles for success, and celebrates his choice to live in a city where he feels alive and energized each day and where he can enjoy outside sports and activities year-round. He also finds additional balance by spending as much time as he can with his wife and young son.

Scott's Tips:

- Embrace the chaos that life presents—that is where you can find opportunities.
- Focus on what you can control, rather than on factors that are beyond your circle of control.
- Be open to continuous learning and be adaptive to change.
- Have a long-term vision, but take small steps each day that will get you to where you need to be. Little steps can create a huge impact over time, like the power of compounding in finance.
- Integrate the things important to you so that you create a way of life. No matter how busy Scott is at work, he still exercises every day as a way to balance body and mind—even holding business meetings on runs!
- Trust that it takes time to get results and that hard work each day will pay off over time.
- Be consistent in your efforts and you will succeed.
- Read biographies of successful people and adopt characteristics that resonate with you.
- Give back. Scott has set up a scholarship fund via his business.
- When times get tough, continue to take good care of yourself and trust that things will get better.
- Live a rich life in all areas of your existence.

Big Dreams, Big Vision

Jordanna Petkun has always been driven toward her goals and been someone who was not satisfied by the traditional path. She would find herself getting bored in more typical jobs, so by the time she was twenty-seven, she knew there had to be something more for her. At this time, she began to recognize her true self-worth and realize that she could accomplish absolutely anything she wanted.

She credits her ability to dream and think big to having been raised by a mother who never questioned and always supported whatever grandiose project either Jordanna or her siblings wanted to take on. It was instilled in Jordanna that any dream or desire is possible. The issue lay in simply figuring out what her next dream was. "If I can create anything I want," Jordanna kept asking herself, "then how do I figure out what it is I want to create?"

Jordanna took advantage of this opportunity to do some intensive soul searching and began to find answers to even the most difficult questions. For approximately six months, Jordanna kept asking herself the same question about what she wanted to create, as well as mulling it over with friends and family. She did this until one day, while on the phone with her mom (her greatest confidant and supporter), Jordanna had what she refers to now as "the lightbulb moment," which turned out was generated from her mom but helped Jordanna to finally flip the switch to turn her lightbulb on.

With this insightful and inspirational moment, Jordanna jumped to action. It became clear to Jordanna that she would open an art center—and not just any art center, but something much larger than anything she'd ever seen before. She had been dancing pretty seriously throughout her twenties and had been surrounded by art her whole life. Even without prior experience in building a business, Jordanna was so passionate about her dream that she knew she would learn and do whatever it took to make her dream a reality. Within a few months, Jordanna had transitioned from teacher to entrepreneur.

Jordanna is now the founder and CEO of Emerge Art Center (http://www.emergeartcenter.com/), a for-profit creative arts center offering classes in all genres of art for adults and children. Remaining positive against what many thought wasn't feasible, Jordanna has stuck true to her vision of opening a 7,500-square-foot center. Jordanna is surrounded by a community full of supporters, a devoted management team, and investors, all who believe in Jordanna and her vision.

Jordanna is a perfect example of someone who has gone the extra mile to make her dream a reality. She has worked multiple jobs while she built her dream. She also has truly believed in herself and trusted her gut along her journey. Jordanna shares that once you're in alignment with your true purpose, you no longer have to spend all that time mulling over the next step—it just presents itself to you. Being in alignment has allowed Jordanna to grow her business concept from a local project to an international project, all before she had her first round of funding. It has allowed her to branch out and become an author and a speaker and a consultant on issues Jordanna is truly passionate about. Jordanna wakes up every day with energy and enthusiasm knowing that she will be doing what she loves to do.

Jordanna's journey has not come easily, but she states that it has been worth every doubt and every struggle. She has dealt in some way with every single item listed as a potential challenge in Chapter 1. It has been a journey full of evading the doubts, jealousy, and concerns of others; of working tirelessly all in the name of her business; of faking it 'til she made it; of facing rejection; of embracing her own craziness; and of knowing that it would be like amputating both legs if she were to walk away from it all. Jordanna says, "When you have found your purpose, you know, and it all becomes worth it."

Life-changing Event Leads to Pursuing His Passion

Michael Koji Spengler was sitting in an airplane on the tarmac, waiting to depart on yet another New York sales trip, when a plane hit the World Trade Center. In one surreal instant, his life was dramatically altered.

It was this tragedy on 9/11 that brought Michael to the realization that he wanted to live his life to the fullest, when so many had needlessly lost their lives. Michael was successful, but not happy, as an international executive. He basically had followed in his father's footsteps of being an executive in a large company, but he knew deep down that his father's path was not necessarily his own passion. The constant travel kept him away from his family and a change was in order. A talented photographer, Michael had dreamt for years that he would one day turn his passion into a career, and this turn of events served as the catalyst he needed.

Michael began taking photographs as a youth in Munich, Germany, where he was raised by his German father and Japanese mother. He studied photography there in his teens and continued his studies in Seattle, Washington, where he lived with his uncle, a professional photographer. He also worked with sports photographers for the University of Washington and staff photographers for the *Seattle Times.*

In 1990, Michael moved to San Diego to attend the University of San Diego, where he served as the photo editor of both the yearbook and the university's weekly newspaper. At the time, Michael had the desire to study fine arts but was told that it wasn't a practical path, so he put his dreams on hold. Upon graduation, he returned to Munich at the request of his father to work for the family's graphic arts printing company, all the while continuing his work in photography in his spare time.

Michael returned to San Diego in 1994 to work for another graphic arts company, developing the first 50-inch ink jet printer, now considered standard equipment for designers and print shops. Later, he moved on to an executive position with a local Fortune 50 company and continued his photographic education through UCSD, the West Coast School of Photography, and other professional programs.

Then, in the wake of 9/11, and after an extremely successful, yet less fulfilling, eleven-year career in the international high-tech arena, Michael was driven to follow his dream. Through working with a life coach, Michael discovered that he truly was meant to follow his lifelong dream of photography. He began to network around town to find out about opportunities and discovered the need for a photographer. Based on this information, Michael gave notice, sold the luxury cars and house in the hills of La Jolla, and dove into the family savings to make his dream a reality.

Michael pursued an apprenticeship with Bill Keane of Keane Studios and Mike Barth of Mike Barth Photography. Upon Barth's decision to retire, Michael became the proud owner of the Mike Barth Photography studio, La Jolla's premier photography studio for over thirty years. After building the business and updating all of the equipment, services, and products, he changed the name of the studio to studio m / michael spengler photography, revitalized all of the marketing materials, and moved the business to a prime location in the heart of La Jolla.

Michael shares that the journey of developing his dream business was not always easy, and he encountered obstacles along the way. However, Michael was very fortunate that Bill Keane served as an outstanding mentor, handing over clients and providing equipment for Michael's studio, business advice, and guidance and support. Michael attributes a lot of his success not only to Bill's availability, but also to being surrounded by a incredible support team that includes his wife, who is a public relations and marketing expert, his father-in-law, who has substantial business experience, and a friend who is a CPA for a major corporation, who was able to help them crunch the numbers and make decisions to make the business viable among competitors.

As his journey began, friends and family weren't convinced that he could pull it off and were pleasantly surprised when he did. What fueled his desire to succeed was an intense need to never return to the corporate world, be in control of his schedule, and live his passion. Michael has done what it takes to keep his dream alive, including working around the clock when necessary.

All of studio m's business now comes from referrals due to Michael's commitment to excellence and personalized attention to the customer. Michael and his work, called "the moment of cool," were recently featured in a cover story of *Professional Photographer* magazine, the national publication of Professional Photographers of America.

In the rare moments when Michael is not in his studio or on location, he spends time with his wife, Jennifer, and their three small daughters, Kyra, Mila, and Evan. He also enjoys staying abreast of the constant and thrilling changes in digital design and printing and soaking up the sunny days on La Jolla's beautiful beaches. Michael says that he often gets caught up in the day-to-day details of the business, but his wife reminds him to reflect back and take a moment of gratitude that he is now living his dream. Michael advises others to not put their dreams on hold or wait until a major event happens to live your dream—pursue your dream now!

International Investment Banker Turned Social Worker

Azim Khamisa is an amazing example of someone who has taken a life-shattering experience and has changed it into an opportunity to live his passion and serve others. Azim was a successful international investment banker, but his life was radically changed when he lost his only son, Tariq, in 1995 to a senseless, gang-related murder. Tariq was a college student at San Diego State University and worked weekends as a pizza deliveryman. He was lured to a bogus address, where he was killed by a 14-year-old gang member in a gang ritual. To honor his son Tariq's life and to find meaning in his death, Azim established the Tariq Khamisa Foundation (TKF) (www. tkf.org) in October 1995. Remarkably, Azim Khamisa reached out in forgiveness to Ples Felix, the grandfather and guardian of Tony Hicks, his son's assailant. Ples joined with Azim in dedicating their lives to ending the plague of youth violence in the United States. Together, Azim and Ples have spoken to tens of thousands of school children through TKF's Violence Impact Forum (VIF) program about the power of forgiveness to break the cycle of violence.

In addition to TKF, Azim is an author and inspirational speaker (www.azimkhamisa.com), where he touches and changes many lives by sharing his journey. Azim has spoken in person to half a million children, with another twenty million being touched by his message through video presentations. The public has also heard his message through print, audio, video, and television specials. A recipient of fifty prestigious local, regional, national, and international awards, Azim's focus remains on his vision of a peaceful, nonviolent world where people make empowering choices. Azim and TKF's work have received numerous awards. In 2002, Azim received the prestigious "Search for Common Ground" international award for "building peaceful communities," along with Archbishop Desmond Tutu and Ted Koppel. In 2004, he participated in the Synthesis Dialogues with His Holiness the Dalai Lama. In 2006 he received the Circle of Courage award from Reclaiming Youth International. His profound work has been featured in the *New York Times, People* magazine, *Parade* magazine, the *Washington Post,* and *U.S.A. Today,* as well as on *NBC Nightly News,* NBC's *Today Show,* and NPR's *Fresh Air.*

Azim shares that we all have defining moments in our lives similar to what Azim experienced, where we can make a choice to be transformed and chose to do something that serves a purpose larger than ourselves. For Azim, he actually views his transition from investment banking to what he does today as a step up in his career. He truly believes that he has found his purpose and finds what he does much more rewarding than when he was an investment banker. What is incredibly rewarding about Azim's journey is that he has been able to leverage his business skills to create success with TKF and his own business.

Azim shares that it is important to ask yourself these three questions when it comes to decisions:

- Does it make sense?
- Does it feel good?
- Is it inspiring?

When we are inspired we are able to achieve remarkable goals, because, Azim states, that inspiration is a far more powerful force than intelligence and emotion. It is important to take the time to be very quiet and listen to what inspires you, trust what your gut tells you, and go in that direction.

> ## Azim's Core Values
>
> - Walk your talk.
> - Practice integrity, forgiveness, and compassionate confrontation.
> - Go to the extra mile.
> - Underpromise/overdeliver
> - Take pride in your workmanship. Make sure everything that you create is quality.
> - Become a qualitative person—have quality in all areas of life, such as the thoughts you have, the food you eat, the people you are with, and the movies or programs you watch.
> - Work smarter, not harder.
> - Be generous with your time and money.
> - Find your purpose by asking how can you best serve others.

From Inspiration to Volunteer to Dream Job!

When Donna Pinto's boys were three and five years old, she found herself longing to reconnect with a side of herself that had taken a backseat to her role as "mommy." Now with both children in school, Donna began to contemplate the interests and passions that had been dormant for a few years. This is about the same time she rediscovered the library! In one year, Donna read over fifty self-development books and listened to about twenty-five inspirational speakers on CD. After hearing the heart-wrenching speech given by Azim Khamisa (whose story was highlighted previously) at a conference called "Awakening A Global Vision," Donna had a revelation.

Azim's speech touched a nerve with Donna. Listening to Azim describe how he transformed his deep despair into forgiveness and healing was the most heart-opening experience for Donna. As the tears poured out, she said she was able to see that everything that had happened in her life—the good and the bad, the tragedy and the triumph—had all brought her to this moment. Suddenly an ocean of gratitude washed over her. It was as if her true calling in life was being revealed to her loud and clear—as though for the first time, she could see and hear the beautiful gift of knowing her life's calling being given to her.

It is a gift available to all who allow themselves to feel deeply and to see that there truly is mystical meaning in everything; to then take action for something because you are compelled to do so—called to give of yourself and live for a higher and grander purpose; to not look away, but rather to look deeply and to feel deeply—this is where it is possible to find your calling.

In an instant it became crystal clear to her. Donna said, "I knew that I had to step up and be a leader—an example for my children, for other children, and for parents everywhere. I could no longer sit idly by on the sidelines." To quote Mahatma Ghandi, "I had to be the change that I wished to see in the world." Although Donna felt proud and privileged to be a stay-at-home-mom, she knew that there was something more that she needed to do.

Eager to put her insights and feelings into action, Donna filled journals that had sat empty for years with new and exciting ideas and visions within a few weeks. She suddenly felt like some kind of powerful force was pushing her. She surrendered to it. After years of not writing, Donna now felt surges of creativity, energy, enthusiasm, and passion. Ideas flowed effortlessly.

Donna soon found herself emailing the director of her son's preschool an idea and a page of notes for an international peace camp. This became the school's six-week summer camp theme, called "Passport to Peace."

Almost immediately after hearing Azim's story, Donna started volunteering the very little child-free time she had with the Tariq Khamisa Foundation (TKF). Witnessing the reaction to one of their grade school assemblies was life-changing for her. She thought, "Everyone needs to hear this story." And three years later, Donna continues to write and share Azim's story. She has found success and fulfillment writing sponsorship proposals, grants, newsletters, and press releases for TKF, as well as for other nonprofit organizations that empower children to make their communities and world a safer and more harmonious place for all.

Donna is thrilled that she discovered how to translate her skills, talent, and passion for writing into a part-time freelance career. She loves being a stay-at-home mom, but she also really loves using her writing skills to help make a difference on a broader scale. She uncovered this by opening her heart, listening to her intuition, and believing she could help make a significant difference. She began by volunteering—taking her three-year-old son to the TKF office and asking how she could help. Slowly, through time and earnestness, she began to learn everything about the organization. One of her first volunteer projects was to go through thousands of letters students wrote after experiencing a TKF school assembly, where they learned of the tragic story of gang-related violence and how it affected the families. These letters expressed the real feelings of children affected by violence and how much they appreciated an organization like TKF sharing its story in hopes of ending the cycle of violence. She began to ponder her skills and how she could help in a bigger way. She asked the executive director and program director lots of questions. Donna also inquired about fundraising programs and became a real advocate and champion for the organization. Once Donna's son started preschool and she had a few extra hours a day, she began to spend more time at the office. Donna investigated where there was a need and offered to seek sponsorships for an upcoming event on commission only. This was basically an offer the executive director couldn't refuse—she had nothing to lose and all of Donna's energy and enthusiasm to gain. Thus Donna's dream career began as TKF's director of strategic alliances.

Walking Away From It All

Frank (a pseudonym) was on his path to becoming a lawyer. It seemed to him a clear path as he studied communications and participated in national speech debates—isn't that what everyone did with these skill sets? After he graduated, he took the next indicated steps and worked in the legislature in Sacramento. It was a dream job. He had lots of responsibility, he met lots of interesting people, and he was in an upwardly mobile position with a clear future ahead. "Why," he asked himself, "does this not feel like enough to me?" When he searched for the meaning, he realized that he had been fortunate to have what he would call an easy life, and he really felt the need to be challenged, even though he already taken a challenging semester abroad to Indonesia during college, where he was evacuated by the Indonesian military during the attacks on September 11, 2001. Something inside of him said, "I've got to try a different path." He thought that by challenging himself, he could truly figure out who he was and what he was made of. So he did what a lot of thought of people thought was insane—he walked away from it all and decided to work in a deli to save enough money to travel to Latin America with his friends. Sure, he experienced self-doubt, thinking, "What am I doing walking away?" But the desire inside of him to try something different was too strong to ignore.

Frank and his friends each bought a one-way ticket to Latin America—not sure when they would return, just knowing that they wanted to be open to wherever their experiences brought them. Their starting point was a language school in Ecuador so they could get their Spanish up to speed. Being open to opportunities, Frank and his friends found themselves working with a public hospital in Ecuador helping children who were suffering from multiple diseases. Frank said that the experience may not have changed the children's lives, but it definitely changed his. They also assisted an animal rescue center in Bolivia, where animals were rescued from being illegally shipped overseas and, most likely, were destined to die a terrible death, such as suffocation, in transit. Frank then found himself working in Peruvian shantytowns. Why did all of this change Frank's life? He realized that he could combine his love for policy with making a big difference in the world to effect change. He found himself asking questions such as, "Why doesn't the Ecuadorian government have better systems in place for health care?"

After ten months of living in Latin America, Frank and his friends returned home to the Unites States with more clarity about their next steps. Frank chose to apply to graduate school to focus on international politics and now is off to serve as a Presidential Management Fellow with the United States Foreign Service in Washington, DC, focusing on East Asia security issues. He never regrets his decision to walk away from what seemed to be the clear and easy path, and in fact, he sees a lot of his previous colleagues feeling somewhat trapped and unfulfilled on the path he once was on. Frank is happy that he listened to that inner calling and made a choice to challenge himself, which got him in touch with a passion waiting to be uncovered.

Adjusting Course to Make a Bigger Impact

Something inside of Tami Walsh snapped. She knew she couldn't counsel one more school-aged girl who had been molested by a family member. She knew she couldn't look at the pain and fear in yet another innocent girl's eyes. And she knew she couldn't take another day of feeling defeated.

Tami had always wanted to support and inspire teens. Her own teen years had been some of the toughest times in her life and she wanted to help improve the quality of their lives and the content of their experiences. At a very young age, before finishing graduate school, Tami had that chance. She was recruited to work in one of the toughest neighborhoods in Los Angeles, counseling kids and teens who were beaten down by life, by their environments, by opposing gangs, and for the most unfortunate, by their very own family members. Tami naively jumped in and believed she could make a real difference as the school counselor for these vulnerable kids and their families.

Tami believed that she would find a way to end the violence. She would create a means to end their suffering. Tami felt that she would bring light and love into the darkness and make the necessary difference she felt called to make. Daily, Tami would go to her windowless office at the school and wipe the painful tears of kids whose parents had been shot in gang-related violence, attend funerals, run grief groups, pull kids off the streets and get them into their homeroom class, and find sponsors to bring money and after-school programs to help put a temporary smile on the students' faces. Tami worked seventy hours a week in a beaten-down environment in a school with over twelve hundred students and no windows in any classrooms. And during the intense six years she worked there, Tami probably went out to lunch twice. She ate her breakfast, lunch, and dinner at her desk daily, and she "lived, ate, breathed, and slept" her job. She was young, naive, passionate, and totally committed to the families and kids she served. Tami developed supportive relationships and a deep affinity with these wonderful people she grew to so deeply care for.

One day in late September, Tami was summoned to room 209 to discover a fourth-grade girl curled in a ball in the corner of the classroom. She wouldn't talk to anyone, and she wouldn't look at Tami, talk to her, or listen to her. She was frozen and ashamed, embarrassed, and alone. She needed help more than any other child Tami had seen. After two hours of reassuring her and coaxing her out of her fetal position and then carrying her back to her office, Tami came to discover that the girl had been sexually abused by her uncle. In that instant, Tami truly believed that she had failed. She felt that she failed this girl and all the others in the community who would be abused in the future. She was working so hard but not succeeding. All her long nights at her desk amounted to yet another girl whose future lay in the California foster system. She'd have to leave the school she had grown to count on and end up who knew where? It was that night that Tami broke down and got into her own fetal position and cried a river of tears. When she emerged, Tami knew she needed to dramatically adjust her course; she just wasn't sure how.

Tami went back to work, day after day, week after week, and though her body was there, her spirit was searching for what was next. She felt the intuitive nudge to quit her job and create a new path for herself. She just really didn't know how or what she was supposed to do with her life. It was a scary and insecure time—she knew she was being forced to emerge and grow, and, for the first time in her life, she hadn't a clue how.

Tami did some deep soul searching and sought counsel and then bittersweetly announced her resignation. She felt instantly relieved and blessed. Tami was clear that going forward she was to be proactive with kids rather than being reactive. She had to get to kids *before* they were in gangs and beaten down by life. Tami had to create a path of hope, of opportunity, of support, and of lasting change.

Again, though excited, fear and confusion took her over. She didn't know how to create her path to change. She began to feel some fear as she remembered that she had been one of the highest paid counselors in the state of California, who now didn't have a paycheck but who had a vision, albeit blurry. It was something to shoot for—something to believe in.

Again, Tami began to feel inspired, excited, and hopeful. But the exact *what* and *how* were missing. What would she get up and do everyday? How would she make that proactive difference with youth? And how would she get paid to do so? Tami had a degree in school counseling but no longer wanted to work in the confines of the school system. What was she to do? She may not have been clear about the exact *what* or *how*, but in her gut she believed she could forge a path that was new and different. She was scared but excited, nervous but eager.

So, Tami took massive action. Being idle was making her crazy. Within one week of resigning, she hired a life coach, who led her on a journey of self-discovery. Next, she attended networking groups, talked to everyone who would listen to her in grocery stores and coffee shops, and read books that inspired her. And then one night, as Tami was in a session with her life coach, the lightbulb went on, and she asked her, "Diane, how did you become a life coach? What is your training? How did you build your practice?" Instantly Tami knew she liked the work she did and she began to think, "Wouldn't it be great if someone was coaching a teen the way Diane was coaching her? Wouldn't it be amazing to help teens discover their true passions, talents, and abilities and then help them chart a course for their life that fired them up?" And in that split second, Tami knew she would do that. Within weeks, she would become the first life coach in the U.S. for teenage girls. After many years of feeling shut down, once again she immediately felt her entire body light up and experience the joy she had lost long ago.

Tami knew that she had woken up in a big way. She now had a vision but wasn't sure of the exact path. With her own life experience as a teen girl fueling her, along with total conviction and determination, she began to attract amazing parents and prestigious schools who wanted her to coach their kids and students. One by one, she began to do so, and by the end of the third year she started the first life coaching company for teen girls in the United States, Teen Wisdom (www.teenwisdom.com). The next year, Tami expanded and opened multiple offices throughout southern California, appeared on regional and national television, and became a motivational speaker and life coach for teens, impacting more than five thousand teen girls. By 2007, Teen Wisdom had spoken to and positively impacted over ten thousand teens.

It has been a wild and amazing ride for Tami—one filled with absolute sacrifice but ultimate reward. It has been filled with magical moments of seeing teen girls she coached become fiercely unburdened by their problems; become better friends, students, and members of their community; and go for their goals and dreams in an unstoppable manner.

Tami has always referenced one key quote from Confucius that has helped give her the momentum she needed when she needed it most, "The journey of a thousand miles begins with a single step."

This is what Tami now teaches teens. This is the truth of possibility for them. And, as long as she is alive on this planet, it is the truth for her as well.

Tami's Wisdom

- Let go. Trust.
- Take daily action. And *believe* your path is perfectly and lovingly planned. It always is and always will be.
- Stay steadfast—it will be worth it!

Finding the Balance:
Passion Combined with Being a Mom

Stephanie Malcolm graduated with a bachelor's degree in computer science, eager to start her graphic design career. Stephanie had already been interning for a small firm and was hired immediately that summer. She had always been an organized person and saw that the office needed some attention. The tasks of sorting old projects, files, and backing up the computer systems led to clients requesting these services for their businesses, home closets, pantries, and event planning. Yet Stephanie's passion was design, so she worked as an organizer on the side but focused on her career. Experience in the design field gave Stephanie titles such as graphic designer, art director, production coordinator, and office manager. Looking back, she was always creating, coordinating, and organizing things, projects, or people well before the title "professional organizer" was created.

When Stephanie had her first daughter, she decided that she would put her career aside to raise her children as a full-time mother. She soon experienced a loss of identity for this new position. Even though Stephanie was completely in love with her child, she struggled with questions like, "Who am I now? Can we make it financially with one income? Why are cyclical events such as doing laundry, cleaning house, and non-adult conversation not as satisfying as creating a brochure or billboard ad?" She longed for a creative outlet.

When her second child came along, Stephanie thought she was getting the hang of motherhood and also thought that the job description should have stated in this way, "Challenging position requires the following skills: Capable of double-duty multi-tasking; able to be on call 24/7; must be capable of tolerating constant interruption of thoughts, conversation, and sleep; must be loving but firm with coworkers; must keep environment clean and in order for stability and visual appeal; must maintain routines and schedules;" and the list goes on. Stephanie loved her job but definitely needed to express herself in a creative manner.

Stephanie's options were narrow for some sort of outlet when she systematically began to rearrange every room in her little house. That felt good, it looked good, and she wanted more. Since her family lived in such a small space, she purged and organized automatically without a thought. That's when it occurred to her that everyone needs a little visual stimulation and definitely everyone needs organizing. Why not fall back on her side work by starting an organizing service?

So Stephanie spread the word. "Stay @ home Mom desperately needs to get out of the house; can offer excellent organizing and design services for nominal fee." And just like that, she was working and creating for others who needed that kind of attention in their homes, yet she was still committed to her family and her position there.

Now that her children are both in elementary school five days a week, Stephanie can devote her "extra time" to her business, Room by Room, which was launched with the hopes that this business would help her family financially and she could work around her children's schedule. And that dream is fast becoming a reality.

She now has four organizing assistants, two interior designers, and two wardrobe consultants available to service her clients on an on-call basis. Her days begin at 10 AM after dropping her kids off, and she ends her sessions at 3 PM, just in time to pick the kids up from school. In an ideal world she would maintain these excellent hours, but as any business goes, hours fluctuate. Stephanie says when it rains, it pours. Her business has been successful and the experience has been unbelievable. Stephanie feels it is an honor to be invited into her clients' personal lives in order to help them in their area of need.

With the addition of each child, Stephanie has adjusted and grown as a person. Now she is adjusting and growing from this new life as a business owner and mother. Stephanie is grateful and appreciates the journey every step of the way!

Taking-the-Leap Analysis

Now after reading all of these inspiring stories, let's reevaluate your situation and do a little different spin on what we did in the last chapter. Let's take a moment to weigh what you have to lose versus what you have to gain by taking a leap of faith to your passion:

What do I have to lose?	What do I have to gain?

For a downloadable form of this worksheet, please visit www.myeasycareerguide.com.

Be Open to Answers Coming in Unexpected Ways

We often have preconceived ideas of the shape that our journey is going to take, and that cuts us off from the unlimited possibilities that are out there. Be open to answers coming to you in unexpected ways. I am a firm believer that there are no coincidences and that serendipity happens all around us as long as we stay open to it. I've had people magically appear on my journey who have helped me in ways that I have never imagined. Early on in building my company, I met an incredible woman who was an experienced entrepreneur who, out of the goodness of her heart, met with me regularly to help teach me the basics of being an entrepreneur, and I am still grateful to her for the guidance she gave me that got my business off the ground. Also along my journey, additional seasoned entrepreneurs unexpectedly have appeared who have provided me with enormous wisdom and guidance. As discussed in Chapter 8, we need to trust and enjoy our journey and know, as the saying goes, "When the student is ready, the teacher appears."

Outside Voices Versus Your Gut

Take the time to differentiate what your gut is telling you and what the outside voices are telling you. Sometimes the outside voices seem to be logical, but our gut is truly what we need to trust. The bottom line is that we are the ones that know ourselves the best. Here are some tips on trusting your gut:

- Go forward signals—When you think about a decision, does your whole body tell you that it feels right? Do you get goose bumps? Do you get a flutter in your belly? Do you smile just thinking about it? Are you ready to commit to whatever it takes to make your dream a reality, including working two jobs, getting additional training, and anything else? If you answered yes to these questions, you are ready and willing to go forward.

- Move away signals—Your body also sends you signals when your gut is telling you no. Do you feel like you are dragging? Do you feel like you would rather stick needles in your eyes? Does that little voice inside you say, "This just doesn't feel right?" If everything is feeling really hard about this decision and you are continually hitting roadblocks, stop swimming upstream and trust that this may not be the right direction for you.

Trusting your gut doesn't mean that there isn't any fear or doubt involved and sometimes requires a major leap of faith. Trusting your gut means that you are moving toward what feels right to you and having faith and confidence that you will find the resources and people you need on your path to your dream job.

For at least fifteen minutes, find a quiet spot and fill out the chart below.

The outside voices are telling me to:	My gut is telling me to:

For a downloadable form of this worksheet, please visit
www.myeasycareerguide.com.

Journal here about what you really want to do:

Chapter 3:
Market And Sell Your Skills

You have to become the expert on marketing and selling your skills to find your dream job. You have to believe in who you are and what you have to offer to convince others of your value.

In the previous chapters, you have clarified what you want to accomplish, learned about your strengths, and uncovered tools to trust your gut and believe in yourself. You have to be able to differentiate yourself in a competitive market, which is why learning how to market yourself is vital to your success. Remember, when you are genuinely passionate about your career path, your energy and enthusiasm will attract the necessary resources and people you need to find your dream job.

First, you have to develop your spin with these following components:

- **Who you are:**

- **What you want to do:**

- **What you have to offer:**

The point of developing a spin is to be able to present yourself in a thirty-second pitch in networking settings. Now put what you have written above together to create your spin.

Example:

> My name is Marcy Morrison and I am the owner of Careers with Wings. I am passionate about helping other find their dream job through speaking engagements, my book, media appearances, workshops, and one-on-one sessions. My big vision is to produce a television and radio show that will enable me to reach more people and provide them with tools to find their dream jobs.

You can also pose a question at the end of your spin, such as, "Do you have any suggestions or contacts that would help me achieve my goals and dreams?"

What is your spin? Fill it in below:

Get Fired Up

When you are out marketing yourself, it is vital that you are in a positive and uplifted state. The best way to do that is to be focused on all of your accomplishments. Make a list of your proudest moments and explain why they are your proudest moments. These are moments that make you shine, create a huge smile, and fill you with joy when you share them with others.

I know this may sound a little crazy, but I have a ritual that starts my day with energy and enthusiasm. I do a happy-gratitude dance each morning to celebrate everything that is wonderful in my life and to celebrate everything amazing that is coming. I hear some pumped-up music in my head as I do it, but feel free to blast the music and celebrate you and your life.

My proudest moments:	Why do these moments make me proud?

My proudest moments:	Why do these moments make me proud?

For a downloadable form of this worksheet, please visit
www.myeasycareerguide.com.

Target Marketing

Often it makes sense to target our spin to a specific event or interview or when writing a letter. Fill in this chart below to clarify the best way to market yourself for a particular situation:

What specific qualities does this job, event, interview, or other situation require?	What kind of skills and value can I add that are a match?

For a downloadable form of this worksheet, please visit www.myeasycareerguide.com.

Here is a list of other important marketing and selling tools:

- A **portfolio**—Put together a portfolio that includes reference letters from professors, past employers, awards, et cetera. This is an outstanding presentation tool in interviews and also a great item to leave with a prospective employer.
- Business cards—Make sure you have business cards on you at all times.
- Dress for success—Dress professionally for all meetings and interviews.
- Research—Be prepared for each meeting by doing extensive research beforehand and having well-thought-out questions prepared.
- Resume—Take advantage of the career services office at your college or local career center to produce a top-quality resume.
- Interview techniques—Get practice interviewing and learn interviewing techniques.

For more resources, please visit www.myeasycareerguide.com.

Chapter 4:
Build A Support Team

Looking for a job or trying to figure out what you want to do can be discouraging at times. For this reason, it is vital that you surround yourself with a support team of positive people that believe in you. Also, many people get beaten down by life. Maybe you have recently been through a hard time that has given a blow to your self-esteem, such as being laid off, getting a divorce, or struggling with a different situation. Make sure that you are getting support in this area, whether it is from friends, family, therapy, or in some other form. You need to be able to clear this out so you can move forward with energy, enthusiasm, and confidence. You can use your support team to help you build up your self-esteem and focus on your strengths and accomplishments. We all have unique and wonderful abilities. Our support team, mentors, and coaches can help us pull them out and truly allow ourselves to shine.

It is completely natural to hit walls while we are on our journey to finding our dream, and there are times when we ask ourselves, "Why am I doing this?" and get so frustrated that all we want to do is walk away. This is where we need to rely heavily on our coach, mentor, accountability partner, Mastermind group, and other members of our support team to pick us up, dust us off, and hold our hand as we walk past the wall. I have found it is often after those hardest moments that something magical happens, that what we have been waiting for—the job, the contract, the contact—was just on the other side of that wall. Had we given up and walked away, we would have missed out on a golden opportunity. I have had many opportunities like this and have been truly grateful for my support team along my journey, who helped me keep believing in my big vision and provided me with the strength to continue.

You can seek out a mentor via your networking, which we will discuss in the following chapter, or find someone who is successful in your dream-job field. If you are unable to find a mentor, consider hiring a professional coach to help you achieve your dreams. Mentors and coaches are crucial in helping you in many different areas, including uncovering areas of weaknesses and providing suggestions on how to overcome or work with them. In addition, seek out inspirational people who have accomplished feats that you thought were impossible. Reading biographies can serve as valuable information and can give you a roadmap of how to achieve your dreams. For example, reading *Leaving Microsoft to Change the World* by John Wood was a huge inspiration for me and proved to me that anything is possible when your heart is in the right place, and you are following your gut, focusing on solutions, and dreaming big.

In terms of your support team, it is important to surround yourself with people who are positive, truly believe in you, and support your dreams and goals. Also, as we discussed earlier, it is really key to have an accountability partner or someone you can check in with at least once a week throughout this process so you can keep each other on track. You could also consider setting up a support group of friends that meets or speaks by phone or that emails regularly to check in with each other, share successes, and ask for help in areas of concern. You can set up a Mastermind group, which is described in detail in Jack Canfield's *The Success Principles* book. I belong to a Mastermind group. We meet once a month, as well as regularly check in with each other via email, to discuss our victories as well as our challenges and to provide support for each other. Belonging to a Mastermind group has been instrumental to my growth and to the quantum leaps I have taken in my business.

Consider hiring a coach to help you achieve your dreams. I was fortunate to have the wonderful experience of working with an amazing life coach. By working with this coach, I was able to clarify my purpose in life, which, as you can see from my website, is not only to provide people with wings to help them find their dream jobs, but also to give wings to children and communities so they can rise above poverty. The coaching experience radically changed my life. Once I was clear on my purpose, I was fueled with energy and enthusiasm and arranged my activities and goals around my purpose. Also, it is incredible to see that the right people, partnerships, and resources keep appearing to help me on my journey of living my purpose. It is wonderful and rewarding to be living my purpose every day. I love helping people develop their wings for success, as well as providing wings to children and communities.

During the first year of launching Careers with Wings, I participated in the Jack Canfield Success Principles Coaching, which is a year-long program and is based on *The Success Principles* book. This program allowed me to work one-on-one with a coach to help me be the best person I can be in all areas of my life. The coaching helped me in these areas:

1) Career/Business
2) Finances
3) Free Time/Family Time
4) Health/Appearance
5) Relationships
6) Personal Growth
7) Making a Difference

Why Have a Coach?

Coaches can help you with many of the following critical aspects to reaching your dream:

- Receive an objective viewpoint—a lot of the time a coach is able to see things that you can't (both good and bad) and can help you improve in the areas where you need to grow, as well as help you build upon your strengths.
- Have a support system.
- Stretch to achieve goals that may have previously felt impossible to reach.
- Work through self-imposed and limiting blocks that may have been learned growing up, through relationships, or in some other settings. These old beliefs may be regarding money, skills and abilities, or what you think you are capable of achieving, among many other issues. These beliefs may be so ingrained in you that you may not even be aware that they are limiting you. By working with a coach you can create awareness and learn new ways to have a more successful and happy life.
- Set measurable goals.
- Have accountability.
- Live the most enriched, balanced, amazing life possible.
- Get on the fast track to achieving goals.

The truth is that people who are successful put the time in to make it happen, are committed to their success, and surround themselves with a support team. A lot of the time we have this misperception that people who are successful have had it easy or that life has handed them their success on a silver platter. However, often the opposite is true, as you saw demonstrated in the stories in Chapter 2. Many successful people have had to overcome a lot of obstacles and disappointment, but what made the difference is that they really believed in themselves and surrounded themselves with people who really believed in them. Also, they learned from others who had to overcome a lot to achieve success. I used to have this same belief that others had it easier; however, the more I read and talked to others, the more I realized that people with even bigger obstacles than I ever had were able to overcome enormous odds and accomplish almost unimaginable feats. For amazing stories, I again would recommend reading *The Success Principles* by Jack Canfield.

During your job search, you will more than likely receive more no's than yes's. It's important to put more energy focusing on the yes's and less on the no's that you receive. Again, this is an important area to leverage the encouragement of your support team. At the same time, use the no's as opportunities to learn how you can do better the next time. When possible, contact the interviewer and ask for feedback on what you did well and the areas where you could do better. Take action on the comments, which may include how you handled yourself in the interview or the fact that you may need to gain additional knowledge and skills. Perhaps the no had nothing to do with you at all; maybe they had a hiring freeze, hired someone internally, or had some other reason.

Who is Your Support Team?

Identify at least ten people who will do the following:

- Give you honest feedback
- Support you
- Challenge you
- Believe in you
- Be there for you
- Have the time to support you

Your Support Team:

1.

2.

3.

4.

5.

6.

7.

8.

9.

10.

11.

12.

13.

14.

15.

Chapter 5:
Network

Networking is the key to finding your dream career. I can attest to this since most of my jobs and opportunities have come through networking. However, before you begin, it is very important that you have worked through the previous chapters to be prepared when you are networking.

When networking, make sure you can articulate what you want to do and what you have to offer in the thirty-second spin that was discussed in Chapter 3. Give your talk with genuine enthusiasm and excitement. Remember to smile, make eye contact, be confident, and listen to what the person you are talking to has to say. Keeping your pitch short is vital; people don't have time to listen to long-winded stories. Also, when presenting in a networking situation, remember that this is not an interview. It is better to make this time more about having a conversation with someone and taking the opportunity to get to know them. Don't force the situation; allow your pitch to naturally work its way into the conversation.

You need to be prepared to present your spin anytime and anywhere. The perfect contact to your dream job could be the person either in front or behind you in line as you wait to buy coffee, with you on an elevator, flying on the same airplane, or walking down the street. For example, during my undergraduate years, my dream was to work at the Council on Foreign Relations in New York City, and I made it a point to let everyone know with my thirty-second pitch. (Sometimes it helps to have a big mouth.) The next thing I knew, a professor at my school who was friends with the President of the Council of Foreign Relations had written a letter on my behalf. It was the key to landing my dream internship. At first giving your pitch may seem uncomfortable, but practice being at ease about talking about your dreams. The more seeds you plant, the faster your garden will grow. Make sure you ask for at least three more contacts when you are networking. Send an immediate thank you note, keeping in mind that a handwritten note is always well received.

Often, attending events can be an expensive but critical way to meet people in your dream field. Contact the event organizer and see if they need volunteers. If so, take advantage of this golden networking opportunity. Be willing to do whatever the organizer wants and be happy doing it. You will be amazed at how this will pay off.

Another fantastic place to network is via your alma mater's alumni network. For the most part, alumni are happy to help other alumni. Contact your school for more information on how to connect with alumni in your dream field.

The amazing part of networking is that often we are surrounded by the exact people who can open doors for us, but they don't know how to help. Once you are clear on your spin, you will be amazed by how much the people around you can help you. I can provide you with two stories. During a session with a client, we determined her passion was global women international policy issues and that she wanted to work in Sacramento. She sent this goal out to her whole network. It turned out that a friend of her mother could connect her with an internship exactly in this field and based in Sacramento. Another client mentioned that she would love to work with kids and in sports and felt that she had no network. As we dug deeper, it turned out that the best man in her wedding was an NFL player! Could there be a more perfect contact?

Once you are clear on the previous exercises, send your spin out to your entire network that you identify in the exercise below. You never know who may be the right person.

Sample Email or Letter to Send to Your Network

Date

Dear X:

I have worked through *Finding Your Passion: The Easy Guide to Your Dream Career* and it had the excellent suggestion to reach out to my network to ask for your support on my career journey. I have identified that I would like to work in (insert your spin) and would love your support in identifying contacts and companies in line with my dream. I greatly appreciate any help that you can provide.

With much thanks,

Name
Phone
Email

Your Current Network:

Contact:	Date Contacted/Notes:
Parents/Siblings 1. 2. 3. 4. 5.	
Relatives 1. 2. 3. 4. 5.	
Job Contacts—Past and Present Employers and Colleagues 1. 2. 3. 4. 5. 6. 7. 8. 9. 10.	
Professors 1. 2. 3. 4. 5. 6. 7. 8. 9. 10.	

Friends 1. 2. 3. 4. 5. 6. 7. 8. 9. 10.	
Alumni 1. 2. 3. 4. 5. 6. 7. 8. 9. 10.	
Other 1. 2. 3. 4. 5. 6. 7. 8. 9. 10.	

For a downloadable form of this worksheet, please visit
www.myeasycareerguide.com.

Target Networking—Identifying the Right Opportunities

In addition to your current network, you can build your network via research and by asking your existing contacts. The key here is truly quality over quantity. I often find that people get desperate and try to hit as many events or talk to as many people as possible to find a job as fast as they can. This only creates a ton of anxiety and scattered energy. It is much more important to keep it simple by doing targeted networking, as well as targeted marketing. Think about your passion and goals and target your research to identify the top ten companies, the top ten events, and the top ten people that can help you find or achieve your dream. Do thorough research. When you exhaust this list, you can start over.

Target Network Worksheet

What are my goals/interests?	Who or what are the top ten people/top ten companies/top ten events that meet these criteria?

What are my goals/interests?	Who or what are the top ten people/top ten companies/top ten events that meet these criteria?

For a downloadable form of this worksheet, please visit
www.myeasycareerguide.com.

Networking-at-Event Checklist

As a reminder, let's make sure that you have what you need when going to an event.

Item:	Completed:
Business cards	☐
Your spin, tailored to event	☐
Research done	☐
Questions	☐
Notepad for taking notes	☐
Target list of companies/people to speak to	☐

For a downloadable form of this worksheet, please visit
www.myeasycareerguide.com.

Building and Maintaining Relationships

When networking, remember that building relationships can take time and that you need to gauge how much help is appropriate to ask for. Always give people you talk to the opportunity to opt out of certain help if they are not comfortable. Sometimes it takes time to develop trust. The more someone gets to know you, the more he or she will be willing to help.

Tips for Developing Relationships

- Always ask what you can do to help the other person. It may be something small, but it is a gesture that is always greatly appreciated and builds a reciprocal relationship.
- Always follow up within forty-eight hours with a thank you letter or email. It can be seen as very disrespectful if you don't acknowledge the help and could possibly burn a bridge for future help. Handwritten notes are so rare these days; take the time to write one.
- Stay in touch—share your successes and ask how the person is doing as well. As a general rule, I contact people who have really helped me at least once a year. If it is only once a year, I send them a holiday email or card, give them an update on where I am, and ask them for their update. You will build lifelong friends this way who you can continue to ask for help and whom you can continue to support.

Here are some great questions for networking, informational interviews, and mentors:

1. What kind of additional study and experience do I need to land my dream job?
2. What kind of salary can I expect starting out and as I grow in my career?
3. How did you get to where you are? Ask them for a road map—the steps they took to achieve their goals.
4. Can you introduce me to contacts that would be valuable in finding my dream job?
5. Can you help me develop a plan for landing my dream job?
6. If I am thinking of changing fields, which of my skills are transferable, and how do I market those skills for a different industry?

For more resources, please visit www.myeasycareerguide.com.

Chapter 6:
Enhance Your Current Job

Often, people love where they currently work, but they feel the need to grow and aren't quite sure where to start. The best place to start is clarifying where you want to go. Ask yourself the following questions:

Question:	Your Answer:
What kind of position do I want to have?	
When do I want to advance within the company?	

The next step would be to speak to your manager or to human resources personnel to find out more information about the following:

Question:	Answer(s):
Is it possible to move into this position and what steps do I need to take?	
How long will it take for me to move into this position?	
Will the company reimburse me for the necessary training?	

It would also be helpful to do some networking with individuals currently in positions that you are interested in. Ask them more about their work and what is required. Overall, my suggestion for anyone is to have the best attitude possible in your current position and be willing to go the extra mile. Your efforts will make you stand out more than anything else that you do, as this following story demonstrates.

Having a Great Attitude and
Strategically Planning Your Next Career Move

Steve Wasson grew up with his dad telling him that no job was ever beneath him. When it came to paying bills or making ends meet, you did whatever job was necessary to make that happen and you did it with a good and grateful attitude. That is what Steve took and continues to take with him no matter what job he is doing, whether that is working in a cemetery, moving boxes, or being vice president of a major health care company.

After college, Steve and his friends decided to pack their bags and move from Pennsylvania to San Diego, California. Steve knew if he wanted to keep his dream of living in San Diego alive, he needed to get a job ASAP. He went to a temporary agency, and the next thing he knew, he was moving boxes for one of San Diego's largest health care providers, Scripps Health. Instead of whining that he didn't want to move boxes, Steve was energized and enthusiastic about an opportunity to make money to stay in San Diego. Another piece of advice from his dad that served him well in this situation was to dress the part of where he wanted to be. So, instead of showing up in typical box-moving clothes, Steve dressed professionally to move boxes because he knew he didn't want to move boxes forever. Steve did the job he was given very well and often completed his tasks early and would ask the staff what else they had for him to do. He also took the time to get to know everyone and build relationships. Steve saw a lot of people who expected a company to offer them jobs, whereas Steve's attitude was, "I've got to prove that I am invaluable and create a job for myself," and that is what he did. He went from moving boxes to a full-time position, and even though it was entry-level, Steve was grateful for the opportunity. He knew that especially in the highly competitive health care industry, he needed to start somewhere.

Eventually, Steve started dressing the part for his next job by showing up in suits and networking and creating opportunities for himself within Scripps. In many ways, Steve was faking it until he made it (as discussed in chapter 2), but at the same time, he was constantly building his knowledge base and found ways to truly provide value. He also realized that he wanted to build more skills. He then presented to Scripps that the company would be able to receive more value for his work if it paid for his MBA, and it did. Of course, Steve delivered on his promise and provided more value in his work.

Did Steve encounter some resistance as he climbed the corporate ladder, especially without a health-care-related degree? Definitely, but Steve said he never let the office drama affect his work, nor did he decide to react to it or take part in it. He believed in himself and his abilities and continued to move ahead and do an outstanding job. Steve also kept up his great attitude and never burned any bridges. Steve recognized that, over time, his practical, hands-on experience outweighed an educational degree in health care. In fact, his degree in economics became a differentiator that helped him stand out.

After eight years at Scripps, Steve decided he needed to expand his skill set to avoid being pigeonholed in one area. Through a fortunate networking opportunity, he was connected to MP3.com, an Internet music company. Steve worked with the CFO. Again he was in an industry that he was not familiar with, but he applied the same techniques that he learned at Scripps, and when he left, he was a divisional general manager. Through this experience, Steve realized he wanted to combine his knowledge of healthcare and technology and began to research opportunities. He found the perfect company, RelayHealth, and decided boldly to call the chairman of the board and state how he'd like to work with this company and how his experience would be invaluable. After a few discussions, Steve was invited to join the company. He now is a vice president and runs all clinical solutions for an entrepreneurial division of McKesson, which purchased RelayHealth.

I wanted to highlight Steve's story because it encapsulates ideas discussed in earlier chapters. Steve's story also highlights what is necessary to enhance your current job and what steps to take to get you to your dream job.

Steve's Advice

- Have a great attitude.
- Dress the part of where you want to go.
- Be grateful for the job you have; no job is ever beneath you.
- Create opportunities.
- Don't let not having the right credentials stop you.
- Build relationships.
- Stay positive—even when you come up against resistance.
- Don't burn bridges.
- Continue to grow and build your skill set.
- Be honest with yourself about what you want in all areas of your life, e.g., your career, where you want to live, and the lifestyle you want to have.
- Set boundaries at work to have balance.

An example of moving up within a company comes from a client who was working in the construction industry on the manual labor side and wanted to move into management. At first, he thought the only way to advance was to change companies; however, the more we spoke, the more it became clear to me that he really enjoyed working for his current employer and that his employer highly valued his work. I encouraged my client to speak to his manager, which led to the client's transition to management. Sometimes that is all that it takes—the courage to ask.

Weighing Your Options

Sally Martin kept thinking she wanted to go into teaching. After working through *Finding Your Passion*, it dawned on her that her current job as a very senior flight attendant was a dream come true. She was reminded that this is what she saw herself doing as a child. Sally evaluated her current situation as the mother of two young children and realized that her job gave her the flexibility, freedom, and financial means to have the lifestyle she wanted as a mom. Going into teaching would have required more schooling and more hours, a sacrifice she was not willing to make after doing some soul searching. How did Sally come to this conclusion? She did a list of pros and cons of both options and came up with her conclusion. Before you jump ship for what *seems* to be a better situation, do this exercise yourself. Afterward, you will be clearer about what is the right decision.

Option 1—Current Job

Pros:	Cons:

For a downloadable form of this worksheet, please visit
www.myeasycareerguide.com.

Option 2—Next Job/Opportunity

Pros:	Cons:

For a downloadable form of this worksheet, please visit
www.myeasycareerguide.com.

Journal about which decision feels better to you. Close your eyes and visualize yourself in each situation to help you further with your decision.

Are You Burned Out in Your Current Job?

If you are burned out, how can you reignite your passion within your current job? First, it is important to examine why you are feeling burned out and then brainstorm solutions.

Issue(s):	Possible Solution(s):	Your Solution(s):
I am burned out with my current job.	Examine if your burnout is coming from other areas, such as from a lack of balance in your life. Perhaps you need to change your schedule around. Cut back on your hours if you are working too much; get out to lunch if you are skipping lunch; take regular breaks, interject exercise before or after work; make sure you are enjoying yourself with activities outside of work. If your burnout is truly due to the position, look into changing positions within the company.	
I don't feel like I am recognized for my work.	Take the time to talk with your boss about ways in which you would like to be recognized. If your boss is not responsive, consider talking with someone from Human Resources.	
I feel like a cog in the wheel and that my work has no purpose.	Ask yourself what would make your work feel like it would have more purpose. See if you can create opportunities, keeping in mind Steve's story about being proactive. Have you taken the time to celebrate your accomplishments?	
Other issue(s):		

Chapter 7:
Set Goals and Get Organized

To ensure success in finding your dream career, you need to stay focused and organized. What I recommend to clients is that they set both short-term and long-term goals in each area of their life at the end of each year, including revising past goals. It is important that your goals are in alignment with the big vision you uncovered in Chapter 1. When developing your goals, here are some questions you can ask yourself:

- How do I want all of my relationships to look?
- How am I taking care of myself—mentally and physically?
- Where and how am I living?
- What is the status of my finances? How do I want them to improve?
- What difference do I want to make in my community and in the world?

Setting Goals and Creating a Plan of Action

It is crucial to clarify exactly what you need to do and when you need to do it by setting specific dates to your action items. Here are some examples below. There is room for you to add your own action items.

Action:	Date to be Accomplished:
Determine a deadline to find your job.	
If you haven't done so already, do all of the exercises in this book.	
Get Organized/Goal Setting: Create your own tracking sheet or use the one in this chapter to set goals and take notes for follow up.	
Create a vision board of what your perfect job/life looks like.	
Every morning and night, read your spin and look at your vision board. Visualize yourself as already successful and in your dream job. Listen to your gut and instincts. Ask yourself, "What is the most valuable use of my time today?"	Daily
Perfect your spin. Practice saying it with confidence and enthusiasm.	
Send your spin to all of the people in your network and enlist their help in your search. Ask if they can give you referrals and if it is OK to use their name when contacting referrals. When sending your spin, don't send a mass email; tailor it to each of your contacts.	
Get business cards to take to all interviews, meetings, and events.	

Attend as many networking events as possible. Set up a calendar of events you want to attend and set a goal of how many you want to attend per month.	
Put together a portfolio of reference letters that you can take with you to interviews.	
Find a mentor or hire a coach.	
Contact your alumni office. Get a list of contacts of alumni in your field, your desired location, or wherever you want to work. Contact them and ask for their help. Be well-prepared when contacting alums.	
Set up your networks online.	
Other Steps/Actions	

For a downloadable form of this worksheet and more resources, please visit www.myeasycareerguide.com.

Managing Your Schedule

Once you have the big goals determined, it is important to break those down into weekly and daily goals. I generally set Sundays aside. Then I review my week, consider my big goals, break down tasks, and assign them to a specific day next week so that I know I am getting closer to achieving my vision. It is important to look at your week and make sure that you are keeping a balance in all of these career areas:

- Research
- Networking
- Interviews
- Phone calls

Of course, you should also build in other areas that are important in your life, such as health and fitness, relationships, and finances.

Example of a Weekly Schedule

Day of Week:	Phone Calls:	Networking:	Interviews:	Research:	Other Life Areas:
Monday					
Tuesday					
Wednesday					
Thursday					
Friday					

For a downloadable form of this worksheet, please visit
www.myeasycareerguide.com.

Setting goals is a great area to leverage the encouragement of your support team, mentor, or coach, who can keep you accountable for the goals that you have set. Create a tracking system with concrete goals, including specific timeframes and dates for finding your job, and determine what steps you are going to take to make that happen.

Here is a useful form for a tracking system that can be developed either in Microsoft Word or Excel:

Company/Contact:	Action Taken:	Next Steps/ When:	Notes:

For a downloadable form of this worksheet, please visit
www.myeasycareerguide.com.

Dealing with Feeling Overwhelmed

Looking for your dream job requires focus, determination, and persistence. There can be a lot of details to manage at one time and it is easy to find yourself overwhelmed. It is important that you stay focused on what is most essential to accomplish at the time. Keep your schedule manageable by using the simplified tracking and charts that I have created for you on earlier pages. When you are feeling overwhelmed, this is an outstanding opportunity to check in with your coach, mentor, or accountability partner to get refocused and back on track. Also, do what you need to do to feel better, whether that is going for a run, taking a break, sitting on the beach, meditating—anything that will relax your mind and help you hit the reset button. When you are overwhelmed and stressed, you are not going to be presenting the best you. People can sense this tension in interviews and in networking situations, so it is important to work through it with your support team. You want to get back to that place of energy and enthusiasm. It is important to try easy, not hard.

Reexamine your approach in your finding your dream career:

- Are you stressed, worried, or anxious?

If so, change your approach. Turn trying hard into trying easy. What does trying easy look like?

- Approach each day with energy and enthusiasm and with a positive attitude that everything is going to work out.
- Visualize your day each morning as if it were already successful.
- Why is this approach so much better?
- Think about it; if you were an employer or a client, would you want to hire someone that is stressed out, or would you rather hire someone that is filled with energy and enthusiasm?

- When you are coming place from joy and ease in searching for your dream, others will be much more attracted to you and want to help you, as opposed to when you are wound up tight and stressed out.
- From your perspective, life is so much more enjoyable when you come from a place of joy and trying easy.

Celebrate Your Accomplishments

Take the time to acknowledge all of the hard work along the way. While it is great to have a clear image of what you want ahead, take the time to celebrate all that you have accomplished and all that you have done along the way each day.

Similar to the chart that we did in Chapter 1, I recommend doing something similar for your accomplishments. Fill in this chart with photos and words from magazines or elsewhere of your dream job and dream life (if this area is too small, feel free to use a bigger piece of paper or some poster board).

Who have I met?	What are my successes?

What have I achieved that has been beyond my wildest dreams?	What unique skills did I pull from that allowed me to succeed?

For a downloadable form of this worksheet, please visit
www.myeasycareerguide.com.

Chapter 8:
Enjoy and Trust The Journey

We all have our journey through life, and so often it doesn't make sense as we are going through it. But in hindsight, the hardest moments are the opportunities in which we grow and stretch and find out what we are truly made of and meant to do. Again, I can share my experience as an example. You have heard pieces of my journey throughout this book and can see an overview in my biography at the end of the book, but there are other details I will share with you. I hope they will inspire you to think big and act big and will demonstrate how working the principles throughout this book will pay off.

I've have had many moments where I have trusted my gut and defied the logical voices around me. In the beginning of my senior year of high school, I had this realization that there had to be more to life than the senior prom and staying in the same high school. I had this burning desire to expand my horizons. I was definitely influenced by my mom, who was an AFS Intercultural Programs exchange student to Germany in high school. Growing up, I was often involved with AFS and saw the value of living in another country and learning about other cultures. One day I came home and said to my mom, "I want to be an exchange student." Needless to say, she was thrilled, because she knew the invaluable lessons and experience I would gain from living in another country. Since I applied to a program that would have me leave in the middle of my senior year and not return to the following year, the logical voices were saying, "Are you crazy? You are going to miss your senior prom and graduation!" However, my gut and my heart were saying, "You have to go." So I did and followed a non-traditional path as the only person in my class of 450 people to be an exchange student. As you read earlier, I spent a wonderful year in Australia, which was instrumental in uncovering my passion for international work, even if it took until after dropping out of college to figure that out. The seed was planted inside of me and popped through the surface when the timing was right.

As I have mentioned, dropping out of college seemed at the time to be a horrendous situation; however, it led me to my passion of international work. After graduation, my dream was to work in Latin America, saving the world. I graduated in the middle of a recession, so I constantly heard that not only was I not going to find my dream job, I would be lucky to find any job. I didn't let that discourage me. I stayed focused on my dream, and after pounding pavement for three months, believing in and trusting myself, marketing myself, and networking like crazy, I landed my dream job with the Inter-American Foundation, doing grassroots development work in El Salvador. During my time at the Inter-American Foundation, it became clear to me that if I truly wanted to save the world, I needed to learn more business skills. It is challenging to help a woman-run radio station in El Salvador write a marketing plan if you don't even know what that is. While building business skills was important to me, I also didn't want to lose touch with the international side, so I found the perfect graduate school program at the School of International Relations and Pacific Studies (IR/PS) at the University of California, San Diego (UCSD), where I studied international management and Latin America.

Well, OK, the story should be simple enough. I'll apply to graduate school, pack my bags, move from Virginia to California, and start graduate school the following fall. It wasn't that simple, but again I learned another valuable lesson when I received my rejection notice from UCSD. I decided to "reject rejection" as Jack Canfield says in *The Success Principles*. I was determined to go to this graduate program; I knew I could do it and I knew that my background and experience were the perfect fit. Since I moved to California specifically to go to graduate school, no was not an option. This was my time to break out those believe-in-yourself and market-yourself tools. I simply went to the graduate school and asked why was I rejected. The staff told me that my GRE quantitative scores were too low. I said, "I know I didn't test well, but I can do it—how can I prove that to you?" They said, "We will accept you on a contingency basis, but you need to take both a calculus and a statistics class and get A's." I said, "Done deal," and I did it. I share this to inspire you to do the same. Shake off your ego and figure out how you can succeed.

During my graduate studies, I decided to test out the corporate world and get some hard-core business training through internships with Bank of America's (B of A) Latin American corporate finance division and with Qualcomm. A lot of people asked me how I got internships at such prestigious firms without any business experience. My answer again was this: I trusted and believed in myself, marketed myself, and networked like crazy. B of A posted an opening at

UCSD, and I decided that it was such a stretch that it would be great interviewing practice. I never expected to get the position. That said, I went into the interview 110 percent prepared by researching B of A and the specific department that was interviewing. I also looked for any connections I could make. At the time, I was volunteering at the Institute of the Americas and saw that B of A sponsored a lot of events there, so I asked for help from the Institute of the Americas to get information that I could use in the interview. I also focused on all of the strengths that I could bring to B of A and it paid off. They hired me based on my energy, my enthusiasm, my preparation, my knowledge, and my connections at the Institute of the Americas. I would like to add that I interned at the Institute of the Americas for free because I saw a lot of opportunity there to achieve my goals, which were connecting with corporations and working in Latin America. I also recommend that people get as much experience as possible, and sometimes that comes from volunteering for free. However, the payoff can be huge.

The story is similar for my internship with Qualcomm. I knew that Qualcomm was growing very quickly internationally. I saw it as a perfect opportunity to expand my business skills while working internationally. I asked around my entire network to see if anyone had contacts at Qualcomm to help me land an internship. Again, my volunteer experience at the Institute of the Americas paved the way. I found a contact through the institute that led me to my internship with Qualcomm. My internship at Qualcomm led to a full-time job with Qualcomm after I finished my graduate program.

After almost two years of working with Qualcomm, I realized that the corporate world was not for me. I also had the realization that part of me was in this job for the wrong reason. For some reason, maybe because my dad was an electrical engineer, I had this crazy belief that you could only be smart if you had a technical brain.

Eventually I realized that I took this job in part to finally prove that I was smart by working in a technical environment. Through some pretty miserable moments of working in an environment not suited to my natural talents or personality, I uncovered that I was smart and it didn't need to be a "technical" smart. That is why I talk so often throughout this book about living *your* passion, not someone else's.

While I was traveling the world with Qualcomm, I became aware of my desire to specifically focus on Latin America. Well, as fate would have it, the division that I worked with at Qualcomm was purchased by Ericsson, and I and many coworkers were laid off as a result of the buyout. While in some ways it was a dark time, since I had no idea of what I would do next, it was also welcome as a way to find work in an area more in line with my passion. Qualcomm hired an outsourcing firm that helped us figure out our next steps, and again, this was one of the best things that has happened to me. One exercise we had to do was to determine the most important opportunities we wanted in our next job. This is similar to the exercise that I have you do in the beginning of this book. Three desires came to me out of this exercise: working with Latin Americans, having direct client interaction, and traveling regularly. Having this clarity was incredibly valuable, which is why I encourage you to search for clarity using the exercises throughout this book. Again, with this clarity that served as my compass, I began (yes, I know I sound like a broken record, but this is the formula) to believe and trust in myself, market myself, and network like crazy. And guess where I went to network? Yes, my favorite place—the Institute of the Americas. And guess what? When I told them what I wanted to do, I needed to look no further because they had the perfect position for me that exactly fit my desire. It's funny how life is sometimes; we often end up right back where we started from in a very positive way. I loved my job with the Institute of the Americas and worked there until I had my first child, and then I began my next journey of being a stay-at-home mom. I love how Jack Canfield says in his Ultimate Life Workshop that a lot of people don't take the time to hit the pause button in life to reassess where they are and think about where they want to go. I stayed home for three and a half years with my two children, and it was such an incredible time to soul search. During this time, as I mentioned earlier, I realized that my life's purpose is to give children wings to rise above poverty. This realization led me to be involved with many activities, including serving on the advisory board of the Just Like My Child Foundation.

When my second child was nine months old, I realized that I needed more adult time, and guess where I went. You guessed it— back to the Institute of the Americas to work in my old position in a part-time capacity. It was wonderful. I worked with fantastic people and I was able to travel again to Latin America.

But life had something else in store for me. It was during this time that I received a curve ball when I had a falling out with a family member that left me in a lot of pain; again, it was a dark moment that would lead me to some of my life's brightest moments. While doing some strategic planning at the Institute of the Americas, I was introduced to an inspirational speaker, Azim Khamisa (www. azimkhamisa.com). As described in Chapter 2, his area of expertise is forgiveness, which is exactly what I needed to experience with my family member. I ended up meeting with Azim to discuss my story and, unexpectedly, Azim and I ended up working together. I had no plans to leave the Institute of the Americas, but it was an incredible opportunity that I knew I needed to experience. I worked with Azim as a consultant for six months on his speaking business and learned a remarkable amount.

At that time, I didn't see myself either as a speaker or an author, but over the next year, it became clear to me that this was what I was meant to do. As you read in the Introduction, I kept receiving feedback that I was profoundly helping people figure out what they wanted to do with their careers and that I should start my own business. It has been and continues to be one of the most wonderful times in my life to put together all of my talents and strengths in a way that helps others live their passion. I am truly grateful and honored to help you on your journey!

Now take the time to journal about your journey and the reasons why some of the worst things that have happened to you are also the best things. Also write down any other valuable lessons you have learned or skills you have gained on your journey. Feel free to use more paper if necessary.

Now it's time to put what you have learned throughout *Finding Your Passion* into action.

> Remember to follow the steps in this book to find your dream:
> - Believe in yourself.
> - Trust your gut.
> - Market yourself.
> - Build your support team.
> - Network.
> - Set goals and get organized.

Don't hesitate, your dream is waiting!

by Isabella Lamb, age 7

Please do not hesitate to contact me at marcy@careerswithwings.
com if you are in need of more support to give your dreams wings.
Sign up on my website at www.careerswithwings.com or www.
myeasycareerguide.com, where you will find additional resources,
giveaways, and support.

Laugh often, dream big, reach for the stars.

—*Anonymous*

Finding Your Passion Bonuses

Register online at www.myeasycareerguide.com for the following bonuses to accelerate your journey to Living Your Passion Through Your Career:

- Become part of the *Finding Your Passion* network.

- Gain access to an online support community and tools.

- Receive downloadable forms contained in *Finding Your Passion*.

- Read additional inspirational stories.

- View exciting products that will ensure that you are living your passion via your career.

- Find out about upcoming events to enhance your journey.

- Get access to free giveaways, including Janet Attwood's of the Passion Test 100 page article entitled "A Life On Fire: Living Your Life with Passion, Balance and Abundance." This article contains secrets from some of the world's greatest legends that you won't want miss including tips from: Jack Canfield, Harv Eker, Janet Attwood, Brian Tracy, Marianne Williamson, Dr. Stephen Covey and others.

Recommended Books

Assaraf, John, and Murray Smith. *The Answer: Grow Any Business, Achieve Financial Freedom, and Live an Extraordinary Life.* New York: Atria Books, 2008.

Attwood, Janet Bray, and Chris Attwood. *The Passion Test: The Effortless Path to Discovering Your Destiny.* New York: Hudson Street Press, 2007.

Canfield, Jack, and Janet Switzer. *The Success Principles: How to Get from Where You Are to Where You Want to Be.* New York: HarperCollins Publishers, 2005.

Cashman, Kevin. *Leadership from the Inside Out: Becoming a Leader for Life.* Minneapolis, MN: TCLG, llc., 1998.

Shimoff, Marcy, with Carol Kline. *Happy For No Reason: 7 Steps to Being Happy from the Inside Out.* New York: Free Press, 2008.

Wood, John. *Leaving Microsoft to Change the World: An Entrepreneur's Odyssey to Educate the World's Children.* New York: HarperCollins Publishers, 2006.

*Please visit www.myeasycareerguide.com
for additional resources and recommended reading.*

About Marcy Morrison and Careers With Wings

Marcy Morrison is the owner of Careers With Wings (www.careerswithwings.com), based in La Jolla, California. Through Careers with Wings, Marcy is passionate about helping others find their dream jobs via media appearances, workshops, speaking engagements, workshops and training, and one-on-one sessions. Marcy's work has been featured in the media to provide hope, inspiration, and practical tools for job seekers. Speaking engagements include the Junior League, Jaycees, the University of California, San Diego's Alumni Association, Women in International Trade, and the United Nations International Career Day, among others.

Marcy has a diversified and successful career. Her experience includes:

- Right Management career management consultant
- Consultant to the University of California, San Diego (UCSD) Alumni Association to research the development of an alumni career program
- Sales and marketing for inspirational speaker Azim Khamisa
- Development and sales with the Institute of the Americas Energy Program, events for which were held in Mexico, Venezuela, Uruguay, Brazil, and Argentina—Clients included BP, Chevron, Citgo, Ernst & Young, ExxonMobil Exploration Company, JP Morgan, Milbank, Petrobras, SAIC, Sempra, Shell, and many more.
- International marketing with Bank of America's Latin America corporate finance division

- International marketing and competitive analysis with Qualcomm, including work in Chile, Malaysia, and France
- Grassroots development in El Salvador and Guatemala with the Inter-America Foundation

Marcy's experience with training and self-development includes the following:

- Jack Canfield's Success Principles Coaching
- Brian Tracy's Psychology of Sales
- Arielle Ford's Building a Platform
- Life Coaching

Marcy Morrison is passionate about international work, traveling, and living overseas, as well as making a difference and giving back.

Marcy has loved living all of the following experiences:

- Being an AFS Exchange Student in Brisbane, Australia
- Studying at the Universidad de Salamanca, Spain, with James Madison University, where she received her bachelor's degree in international affairs and Spanish
- Studying international management and Latin America at the School of International Relations and Pacific Studies (IR/PS) at the University of California, San Diego (UCSD)
- Volunteering with AFS Intercultural Programs
- Serving on her graduate school's board, where she developed a mentoring program
- Serving on the board of her son's nursery school
- Speaking at a variety of events to motivate and inspire students
- Serving on the board of the Just Like My Child Foundation, Inc. (www.justlikemychild.org)

- Hosting a lemonade stand with her kids and friends to raise over $350 for Room to Read (www.roomtoread.org)

Marcy lives a balanced and fulfilling life that includes these essential activities:

- Time with her husband and two kids
- Organizing fun social events and spending time with friends
- Continued self-development, including reading lots of fabulous books
- Exercising, including horseback riding, biking, running, yoga, and workout classes at the ocean
- Meditating
- Singing
- Learning about other cultures and traveling,

Permissions

Azim Khamisa, interviewed by author

Dominic Catalano, interviewed by author

Sally Estrada, interviewed by author

Bill Hagey, interviewed by author

Scott Kyle, interviewed by author

Paul Lamb, story provided

Vivian Glyck, interviewed by author

Stephanie Malcolm, story provided

Sally Martin, interviewed by author

Stella Medina, story provided

Jordanna Petkun, story provided

Donna Pinto, story provided

Eric Seastadt, interviewed by author

Michael Spengler, story provided and interviewed by author

Joe Sweeney, interviewed by author

Tami Walsh, story provided

Steve Wasson, interviewed by author

BUY A SHARE OF THE FUTURE IN YOUR COMMUNITY

These certificates make great holiday, graduation and birthday gifts that can be personalized with the recipient's name. The cost of one S.H.A.R.E. or one square foot is $54.17. The personalized certificate is suitable for framing and will state the number of shares purchased and the amount of each share, as well as the recipient's name. The home that you participate in "building" will last for many years and will continue to grow in value.

Here is a sample SHARE certificate:

YES, I WOULD LIKE TO HELP!

I support the work that Habitat for Humanity does and I want to be part of the excitement! As a donor, I will receive periodic updates on your construction activities but, more importantly, I know my gift will help a family in our community realize the dream of homeownership. I would like to SHARE in your efforts against substandard housing in my community! (Please print below)

PLEASE SEND ME _____ SHARES at $54.17 EACH = $ $_____

In Honor Of: _____

Occasion: (Circle One) HOLIDAY BIRTHDAY ANNIVERSARY

OTHER: _____

Address of Recipient: _____

Gift From: _____ *Donor Address:* _____

Donor Email: _____

I AM ENCLOSING A CHECK FOR $ $_____ PAYABLE TO HABITAT FOR HUMANITY <u>OR</u> PLEASE CHARGE MY VISA OR MASTERCARD *(CIRCLE ONE)*

Card Number _____ Expiration Date: _____

Name as it appears on Credit Card _____ Charge Amount $ _____

Signature _____

Billing Address _____

Telephone # Day _____ Eve _____

PLEASE NOTE: Your contribution is tax-deductible to the fullest extent allowed by law.
Habitat for Humanity • P.O. Box 1443 • Newport News, VA 23601 • 757-596-5553
www.HelpHabitatforHumanity.org

EAU CLAIRE DISTRICT LIBRARY

Printed in the United States
145872LV00011B/35/P